The Gift of Awakening

Kristen Lee Fewel

To Adriana~
May your AWAKENING
be beautiful!

♡ Kristen Fewel

The Gift of Awakening
Copyright © 2018 by Kristen Lee Fewel

ISBN: 978-1987530933

Printed in the United States of America

CONTENTS

ACKNOWLEDGEMENTS

My heart is filled with gratitude for everyone who made this book possible. I am grateful to my clients, students, and friends who shared their stories with me which contributed greatly to the credibility of this work and lifted its potential to help people navigate this strange and complex world of energywork. My sincere thanks for my parents who brought me into this world and the parents who raised me as their own, my children Shane, Leilani, and especially Noah, my greatest teacher who endured the longest and most difficult parts of my healing journey, and to my husband Jeff for his enduring patience and unconditional love.

Special thanks to Julie Sifter, Vitzania Dominguez, Blanca Karcher, and Susan Davila for their friendship, inspiring spiritual gifts, and for helping me to define my audience and purpose in writing this kind of book, and to all the beloved teachers and students at Full Circle Yoga & Healing Arts for their persistent encouragement. Thanks also go to Patrice Sorokin for her guidance with the title and cover design, and to Karla Noonan and Tim Brittain for polishing my words and images. And finally, I offer deep bows to my personal teachers and spiritual parents, Ariel Hubbard, Michelle Adams, and Ryoko Gibson who know my heart and have always allowed me to be myself.

INTRODUCTION

This is a non-religious self-help book for highly sensitive people experiencing anxiety or confusion that may stem from a spiritual crisis or a spiritual awakening. This book is also appropriate for friends, family and health professionals to support and encourage their loved ones in a non-clinical manner. Spiritual crisis is not an easy topic to discuss or relate to; especially if you don't know that it is happening to you or have never met anyone who has experienced it. It gets even more complicated to communicate about spiritual energies because our language and culture lacks support for naming its very existence. Highly sensitive people are becoming aware of each other more than ever, gathering together to share and support each other's gifts and provide healing to one another. May this book be a resource to help them connect and understand each other better.

I offer practical guidance with the teachings of yoga, mindfulness, and self-care by sharing my unique spiritual awakening journey along with the stories of others who are navigating their own healing journeys. This book is for people who are waking up, as if from a deep sleep or dream, who want to find out why they overwhelm so easily, consumed with doubt and worry, and how to get out of the cycle of suffering. It is also for those who are managing a spiritual awakening well, enjoying increased energy and awareness of the spiritual world, but could use advice on how to use their gifts for greater benefit. Modern life is pushing more energy and information through us too fast as through a time-space portal that highly sensitive people must learn how to moderate for mental and physical health. Sometimes it feels as if we are being pushed or pulled into crisis just so that we can experience the healing journey, and it is no coincidence that it is through this experience that we awaken to our true self. The healing journey is not an easy ride, but it is a precious opportunity to increase our personal power and health through the rest and recovery process.

The stories shared here and my views about spiritual awakening are different from other spiritual self-help sources. I do not promote any particular religious philosophy, nor disparage with any religion. Although I personally believe we are All One with a higher power, it is not a requirement for you to have faith in anything that you have not personally experienced to benefit from this book. In reference to spiritual energy that is not generated by an apparent source I interchangeably use the terms G/god, Higher Power, the Divine, All One, and All That Is. You are welcome to use substitute language such as Higher Self or the Power Within to relate to that which creates, transforms, destroys, and recreates everything in our world. It is my belief that all things are interconnected and the Power will not mind how we choose to speak of it. The feelings and processes of awakening described here differ from person to person, may occur in anyone at any age, and from any land or language. It is my hope that we can transcend the limits of language to shed light on true understanding.

In a world that is operating from a largely programmed and unconscious mind, waking up to find yourself in tune with spiritual energy is absolutely life changing yet challenging beyond belief. I have no doubt that your journey into awareness of your abilities and the healing journey will improve your life, as much as I am certain that it will pose many challenges to you. Spiritual awakening is like being embraced by every atom in the universe, whereas spiritual crisis feels more like being pelted with every atom in the universe. It's beautiful when you discover the purpose of awakening and its benefits, but the process can also leave you feeling lonely, agitated, confused, or in pain. The overall benefits of the awakening and participation in your own healing will confirm that you are on the right path to finding a greater purpose in life. Thank you for coming onto the path; now let's find out what we have in common.

1

INTENTION & ATTENTION

Where attention goes, energy flows;
Where intention goes, energy flows.

~ James Redfield

Most of my experiences as a highly sensitive person with mystical encounters were confined to handwritten journals I began as a teenager. Those journals written long ago were a precious time-capsule of drawings, poems, and letters to my future self in whom I had placed the utmost sacred faith and confidence to one day make sense of how I felt about my place in the world, my connection with energy, and my relationship to God. My journal became my closest friend because it reflected my true feelings, kept my secrets, and helped me find my authentic self. I felt strongly that I would one day have clarity and recall my purpose for being here, and that those immature writings would guide me to understanding my past and provide insight to illuminate my future. I believe that yesterday's ignorance may just be tomorrow's wisdom and compassion which is and has always been at the heart of the gift of awakening.

I was very young when I first received an extra-sensory gift that I did not know how to use. By the time I was in grade school, I had learned that interacting with energies or entities that other people could not see made me appear different. In those early years, I learned to keep mystical experiences and extra-sensory information to myself to avoid further complicating my daily life. I did not bother my actual friends with anything unusual. It was my dream to one day discover a mentor or a group who could validate my experiences of a spiritual world. After years of refraining from being my authentic self in public school, an unstable family, compounded by typical teenage insecurity, I had forgotten about who I really was and I forgot my gift. I started to see myself as separate, different, and somehow impaired or dysfunctional, as someone who does not know how to use the tools everyone else uses to get along in life. During my young adulthood I had some inclination that I was to try to help people, but with mediocre grades and low self-esteem, I was adrift with only the shallow pride of maintaining at least two low-paying jobs to support myself and pay my own bills. I soon tired of chasing commissions and minimum wage, so I looked into using one natural gift I knew I had—helping people feel better when they are sick or injured.

I was drawn to the helping professions, so I took training from a sports medicine clinic as a physical therapist aide and chiropractic assistant which involved deep tissue massage and injury care for their patients. After a year of training with two chiropractors and a physical therapist at the clinic, I was offered a shiny new business card with my name in bold letters and my new career labeled as "Massage Therapist." I felt that being acknowledged in this professional way with a title was an important step toward "becoming" somebody in this world. In the rather touchy-feely field of massage and bodywork there were also good opportunities for me to meet people with extra-sensory gifts when I was invited to metaphysical and spiritual gatherings. I figured that when all the "different" people got into a room together that everyone would feel the same, which was not the case at all! I had no idea at the time that people who are 'different' are also very different from each other.

The 1990s brought the brick-and-mortar boom of metaphysical bookstores and yoga studios where one could learn almost anything on the fringe and openly share about spirituality in small groups and communities. I spent every day off work perusing the self-help, spirituality, and world religion sections in bookstores and libraries. Libraries were my school because I could follow my own interests at my own pace and the best part was that it was free. At a time when I could not even afford a typical yoga studio class, I always had my eyes open for low-cost, donation, or free educational activities or experiences that would feed my self-education.

I took my first yoga training in 2000 by the grace of a small independent studio owner who heard my plea for community and training in yoga studies. The education and support I received in that training group inspired me to one day open my own center. As the world wide web was expanding, I was fortunate to discover virtual chat rooms by the likes of AOL and Yahoo as the first virtual gathering places for seekers of spirituality and metaphysics to find their tribe. Non-religious spiritual groups have always existed, but as connection speeds increased, the growth rate of the tribe and utilization of this powerful spiritual resource also grew. Nearly a decade later, chat rooms gave way to numerous websites and social media groups that mimicked the growth acceleration and information available to connect spiritually curious, spiritually devastated, and spiritually awakened folks, myself included. My self-doubt was no match for what the universe had in store for me, if I could only keep my eyes —and my mind— wide open.

In keeping with my intention to grow my healing arts community, I opened Full Circle Yoga & Healing Arts center in 2010 near my home in Yorba Linda, CA where very few centers of wellness or alternative therapies could be found at the time. My tribe was once on the internet and spread across the land I could not have afforded to travel to, and now my tribe comes to my space seeking spiritual counsel, energywork, healthy lifestyle guidance, plant-based nutrition, and of course, yoga. I often work with beginners who do not know anything about yoga when they come, but I am often told that they were guided here not only by the typical online search results, but a serendipitous sequence of referrals. My center isn't anything like a gym, a temple, or a school, but there are elements of each so that you can experience physical health benefits, spiritual uplifting, and education about how yoga and meditation works. And it really does work! It is really a special thing to find a comforting place where you can discern the external from the internal and find out truly who and what you are.

"It's like coming home," said several clients and students, and when I started hearing that phrase repeatedly from different people over time, I realized that something had taken form in my healing center that I didn't ever have to force—it just happened. When my focus and attention was directed on making connections with good people with light in their hearts, helping each other rise up to shine their light even brighter, the energy flowed easily and more relationships were built. Most of these healing relationships were built one-on-one from teacher to student. Some of those relationships created a special interest in helping to attract people to our center. Some of these people were healers themselves. Others came in with a special need for healing or instruction. Others expressed a sincere desire to learn how to heal themselves and family members which inspired a formal training program in yoga, meditation and reiki energy work. It all came together, person to person, and it continues to grow. As the saying goes, "Where the attention goes, the energy flows!"

Like any other business, I advertise in some traditional ways but word of mouth and the power of positive energy has carried our message farther than I could have imagined at the beginning. There are numerous businesses that are founded on these principles of good energy flow, and it shouldn't come as a surprise that a person will start to make changes in their buying habits when they become aware of stores that are not grounded in good energy flow, with no concern for the wellbeing of the people who work or shop there. One of the changes that occur when we awaken is seeing and knowing things that we could not see before. Imagine how much happier the world might be if everyone followed the good energy to work for and with organizations that help people through good products that do not harm people, animals, or the environment! Our teaching and healing community has grown as the good energy and vibrations have amplified and reached people even if they were not consciously aware of why they needed it.

Although I own a yoga center, I don't push anyone—not even my own family and friends to do yoga, or anything else for that matter. I believe that everyone has to find their own way in life and to resolve their suffering even if yoga is not their way. But some lights shine brighter than others, and when the time is right for someone to walk in the door, they realize why they have come. They are ready to discover their own light. A community of highly sensitive, spiritual people have managed to gather in one of the most conservative areas of the country where I happen to live. My mission is to attract more of us together—virtually and personally—to put our collective wisdom and compassion together, to heal and to help each other locally and globally.

2

SPONTANEOUS AWAKENING

ALL THERE IS

Is this all there Is? Yes.
Is there more? Also, yes.
Is this sad, promising, both?
Mortally, humanly, yes.
The sky is full of wispy, billowy, crisp clouds
and a peek of blue sky.
I breathe it in
I breathe it out
Expanding and contracting with the whole universe
I am a part of it, and it is part of me.
Is this all there is? Yes.
Is there also more?
More, yes.

When I was six years old, I had my first spiritual awakening. If an angel ever kissed my forehead or left his calling card under my pillow the night before, I have no evidence. I lay on my bedspread in the late afternoon summer in 1977 staring at the popcorn ceiling in a peaceful state of complete mindfulness. A warm summer breeze was blowing through pink-and-yellow curtains and a few inches of screened window of this first-grader's room.

Dancing shadows of the backyard citrus tree were moving over the plush dolls, toys, and ballerina-pink walls.

I was a bright and curious child and punishment did little to deter me from exploring my world, so I had been sent to my room to "think about it." Daily I climbed rugged fences and tall trees, talked to perfect strangers and argued with parents and teachers for my point of view. I was often frustrated with adults who had their way while my opinion and feelings were not heard, which I interpreted as a lack of respect. I was not an angry child, but this lack of positive attention in my early formative years led me to broadly disregard most of the boundaries and rules expected for children to follow. I was neither hostile nor unfriendly in any way; I simply behaved in a way that made me feel happy and free and that did not always make authority figures happy with me. It is quite likely that I was sent to my room on this particular occasion for some minor infraction like not cleaning up my toys, singing too loudly in the house, or getting a note sent home from school for excessive daydreaming.

I greatly enjoyed quiet time and "zoning out," which I often did in school no matter how many people were staring or imploring me to answer their questions. Some discouraging terms used to describe my school behavior were "dreamer", a "dawdler," and " a bright underachiever." I had an imaginary friend (in addition to a few real, physical friends), engaged with energies and entities no one could see and was a master of daydreaming. A good amount of my attention in school was focused outside the window, longing to be outside under a tree, playing with rocks, or studying an ant colony in the sand. I also held quiet space for myself and no-thinking for a part of every day, even when I wasn't supposed to.

This particularly ripe occasion of spiritual awakening was most likely made possible by some special conditions that I had not experienced before. These are special conditions most people do not allow themselves in an entire lifetime. Since it could feasibly happen to anyone under the right circumstances, it may help to understand what the particular circumstances were that made this moment possible.

Awakening to Interconnection

Sacred Gates of Awakening are special types of experiences under which a person emerges from a dreamlike state into a sacred way of being, according to Buddhist teacher Jack Kornfield. The Gate of Awakening through Oneness, as Kornfield describes it most closely describes the divine connection I felt during my first spiritual awakening as a child.

Lying there on my bed in my room, I was not upset at anything. I was relaxed, awake, quiet, and I had no expectation of anything: I knew I was going to be there for a while "to think about it," and no one was coming to get me soon. I stared up at the acoustic "popcorn" ceiling with fuzzy vision, observing the space above me without focus on anything that anyone could see with the naked eye. I was present. Everything was stillness and peace. I had no need to do anything. I was neither angry nor excited, or even thinking about the situation that led to my imposed isolation. Within me, all was peaceful and still. Experiencing the curtains blowing, the sun shining into my room, I got a sense that I was being embraced, accepted, and loved by something or someone I couldn't see. This feeling filled my whole being. In that state of pure mindful awareness, I experienced my first spiritual encounter with the Divine as a six-year-old.

At that age I had not been taught to pray and had no memory of ever having attended a church. I had no concrete images of what God would look like or what He, She, or It would say to me. What came to me that day was not an image, but pure Spirit which wordlessly communicated directly into my mind on a level that I could receive its message that All are One. Although I did not know the qualities of God at the time, I had this feeling I was One with God in this direct experience of God. I had never heard nor seen anything about yoga in my life, but this is the day, the very moment, I awakened to yoga: complete absorption in oneness with the Divine.

I knew that underneath every person's appearance were the elements and energies that made up every being in the universe: the clouds in the sky, all the stars and planets, flowers and trees, every human being and animal on Earth, and God itself. I felt calmly reassured by this knowledge of great truth, and knew intrinsically that I was part of a much larger body of existence that I had not yet seen in my young life. I felt a web of universal energy that connected me with every other being in the world, having only seen a globe to comprehend how far that really extended. I felt a wonderful rush of tingling on my skin and in my head, but I wasn't cold. I was completely clear, abiding in that moment with total openness.

This experience was so enjoyable and illuminating that I returned to the same spot at another time to receive more information which came in the form of visions about a past life. I received this as one would recall a "memory," like a biopic movie without the moving pictures. I had my eyes open for a time, but closed them for a bit to see if the "movie" would go away, but there it was playing in short scenes over and over. I realized I was watching myself in this movie, not a character and not a historical figure. This would be like watching a film where the characters do not look like anyone you know, but you can tell without a doubt which actor in the movie is playing you.

I played this vision in my head again and again looking for clues to its meaning. I became so familiar with it that I was able to mentally fast-forward and rewind to the most interesting and revealing parts! The past and present felt like a great constellation of moments for all beings that went on forever in all directions, and I was just a tiny part of all of it. As a testament to my maturity at the time, I didn't tell anyone about my past life vision until I got into high school, where peculiar adolescent thoughts and philosophies shared with friends were perceived as freaky and fantastical stories of imagination. Since I hadn't told anyone for a very long time, I had even begun to doubt my own memory as if perhaps those experiences had never happened.

For a long time this dream-memory of a past life was the only part left from my first awakening that I could remember. It was a thin thread of communication with the Divine that later compelled me to investigate further. Once at a girl's sleep-over party at a friend's house, I was introduced to the Ouija board, a sort of "talking board" with letters and numbers on it. When the participants asked a question and put their fingertips on the sliding indicator, the board would supposedly spell out messages that would give you an answer, or, as the game board manufacturer would have you know, "bring you good luck." The first questions we asked the board were typical of young girls' party games such as, "When will I get married?" and, "Who will be the first to fall asleep tonight?" Some of the girls fought the board to spell out a girl's name while others pushed the indicator to do their own bidding, when our attention suddenly turned to our dead ancestors and mysteries of the afterlife which was the popular opinion in the room of what the game was really about. This interesting and mysterious game made some of the girls scoff and joke. Some got creeped out and said God was going to punish us all and send us straight to hell in our sleep for playing it, but there were a couple of us who focused our minds on receiving guidance from the spiritual world. In turns, we doubted its accuracy and blamed each other for moving the indicator, but at the same time we had a feeling we were being guided, utterly fascinated with the truth and accuracy of the responses we received. Although I'll never know for sure who or what made that game seem so believable, I longed to know more about the energy that moved it.

Awakening to Oneness with God

The profound experience of satori, or awakening, is directly accessible through meditation and mindfulness practice, but it can also arise spontaneously when the conditions are right. Some people claim to be born this way, but many energy-sensitive people awaken from a type of spiritual slumber when something mystical suddenly happens which causes them to awaken to a higher consciousness. This type of experience is so profound that it may change how they think and act, and may feel called to a more spiritual way of living and being. Someone born with this awareness may or may not have been raised with religion, but these special people born with the Divine Light have great compassion and have a natural gift for comforting people and animals.

Some people connect with God through their religion. Others connect with the Divine through nature here on Earth. People who have moved through this Gate of Awareness have a direct experience of God without any sort of leap of faith that most other people need in order to know and experience God. This is not the Gate that a sworn atheist would typically encounter. This is the Gate I first encountered as a six-year-old child in my bedroom, but I don't think it was a coincidence that I was also in a deep state of meditation when it occurred and that I had not formed any strong opinions about what God is at that age. Although meditation does not always lead to an experience of the Divine, the conditions that lead to meditation can also lead us to experience the Divine that is not limited by religion or belief for that matter.

One of the larger truths that comes from awakening to Oneness with God, is that all beings are interrelated and interdependent on each other. His Holiness the 14th Dalai Lama often counsels world leaders with this wisdom to encourage compassionate action toward the environment and in matters of human rights. He reminds us there really is no separation between Self and Other; therefore, Benefit to One is benefit to Others as detriment to One is detriment to Others. You don't have to look far to see how your truths are reflected in harmony or disharmony with your body, your relationships, how you make a living (or what you wish you were doing for a living), how you treat animals, and how you respect (or disrespect) the planet. If or when you awaken to Oneness with God-- which includes your interrelationship with all beings including the planet you live on-- you will face a personal reckoning for the changes you need to make to be in Oneness. This reckoning to be in harmony with your soul and your lifestyle can cause a great deal of anxiety for some people, which takes time, patience, and compassion to occur.

3

SPIRITUAL CRISIS

For a seed to achieve its greatest expression, it must come completely undone. The shell cracks, its insides come out and everything changes. To someone who doesn't understand growth, it would look like complete destruction.

~Cynthia Occelli

Nestled under the burned and blackened scrub brush of the southern California desert lie a special kind of dormant seed known as 'fire-followers.' These are the seeds of once colorful and proliferate plants and wildflowers that have succumbed to the intense heat and smoke of a sweeping California summer hillside wildfire. When the heat from the fire grows closer and intensifies, the plant drops its seeds, leaves curling inward, stems crisping then glowing, the fire consumes the fuel to finally burn itself out to ashes on the ground. In this barren black and gray landscape, it is hard to imagine witnessing the fire in person, or that anything could live or grow there ever again. It looks like complete devastation. But in one of the most fascinating cycles of destruction and renewal, the seeds of the great and fabulous 'fire followers' lay in dormancy amongst the ashes.

No one can predict when the rebirth will occur, but nature knows when the time is right. Up from the ashes will come the pale sunshine-yellow whispering bells, Big-Bird-yellow popcorn cassia flower, long stemmed fingers of fire poppies, wild 'butter-and-eggs' snapdragon, and the long tree-like stalks with their fragrant golden eardrop blooms. The blackened manzanita bushes, charred oak, and crunchy sage now surrounded by living waves of fabulous foliage in popping color stop us in our tracks, and we say, "Wow, this place was charred to waste this time last year, and now look at it!"

These fire-flowers follow a similar path of arising as the ancient Greek myth of the mystical phoenix that transforms itself with fire to consume and destroy what it has been. It cyclically regenerates itself by rising from the ashes to be reborn as a bright and shiny new phoenix. There is a reason that this tale of death to rebirth has been told in every culture of humanity on the planet for all time: it gives us hope. When we are feeling consumed by the world, we can choose to ride into the flames, hunker down for the transformation, and know that we will rise from the ashes with a new perspective—if we are willing to trust the process.

Dr. Gail Brenner shares about coping with challenging life circumstances, "Phoenix rising from the ashes. This phrase popped into my head recently, and I wasn't sure why until I did the research. As the story goes, the phoenix is a mythical bird with fiery plumage that lives up to 100 years. Near the end of its life, it settles in to its nest of twigs which then burns ferociously, reducing bird and nest to ashes. And from those ashes, a fledgling phoenix rises – renewed and reborn. And now I get it. This is the story of my life in the past few months – especially the part about burning ferociously. Life presented me with some challenging circumstances that left me just hanging on. And now, sanity has returned. I look out with fresh eyes. The fog has lifted, and the dark clouds have moved on."

When I was researching and discussing images about emerging from crisis and spiritual awakening, the phoenix came up. But when I heard from a friend about the blooming golden eardrops in our area, and that they were a part of this special group of fire followers, I thought it was a refreshing image that put a new perspective on what is possible following a spiritual crisis. The nickname for golden eardrops is "golden teardrops," for their flower essences are said to assist in emotional detoxification to release painful memories from the past.

After the fiery crisis, there is definitely an opportunity to reframe the process as a kind of rebirth, a beautiful gift of wisdom as an ideal outcome of a spiritual crisis. We have to crack our shell to allow for some undoing of our insides, allowing changes in our perceptions to occur with faith— backed by knowledge through experience— that we will not only recover, but bloom spectacularly! What most people don't understand is that when they are in the midst of a spiritual crisis, despairing the desolate landscape of their life, they fear they may never grow anything beautiful ever again, lacking a reference point of the emerging gift of awakening.

We can learn a lot from observing nature. I found a news article by Steve Scauzillo from the *San Gabriel Valley Tribune* interviewing Rick Halsey, Director of the California Chaparral Institute about how what people expect after a devastating fire is different from how nature recovers. "We look up at the hillside after the Colby Fire and they say it is a moonscape. That is the way it is supposed to be. It is the natural way of things. The Earth has a way of healing itself. Everyone wants to plant trees or make the black go away," Halsey said. "People are impatient. The best thing to do is to accept the fact that this area burned and nature will recover without our interference. We are expecting a phenomenal bloom."

Make no mistake about it. Enlightenment is a destructive process. It has nothing to do with becoming better or being happier. Enlightenment is the crumbling away of untruth. It's seeing through the facade of pretense. It's the complete eradication of everything we imagined to be true.

~Adyashanti

I have studied diverse applications of yoga, meditation,

bodywork, and energywork for more than 20 years. As a yoga and meditation teacher, people come to me primarily for relief of their bodily and emotional discomforts. Among the vast array of healing arts available to us in the west, yoga is one of the most effective ways to relieve the body and mind, but it's not the brand of popular fitness or fad culture. What once was considered a purely spiritual pursuit of uniting with the Divine, or merely as stretching, yoga is the result of calming the mind and restoring our body to balance. Yoga is a mind-body connection, or union, that awakens us to an inner wisdom that is spiritual, but not religious. Consistent, appropriate practice can lead to the normalization of the body's physiology, which has the effect of relieving many of the body's discomforts. Yoga is a form of self-care that can be learned, practiced, and adapted for each person as they thrive, grow, age, and recover from life's unexpected transformations. Yoga has cumulative beneficial effects which at its highest potential can enhance the entire spectrum of human experience—physically, emotionally, mentally, and spiritually.

I first came to yoga as a massage therapist facing the likely end of a twelve-year career because I was starting the feel the strain of the job without having an exit plan for leaving the profession gracefully. It was a physical job which I enjoyed very much, lugging my massage table around providing pain management and palliative care for the patients of chiropractors, physical therapists, sports medicine clinics, and my own private clients. I had a flexible schedule, a sense of profitable livelihood, and a job title I could be proud of despite having dropped out of junior college. My career in bodywork was enjoyable, but I struggled with my own self-worth, having to garner acceptance and praise through my loyal, satisfied clients. I had a habit of moving my office and home every year or two in an attempt to bury a personal conflict when, in fact, I had just created another. I was also on the verge of burning out and breaking down in a mental, emotional, and spiritual crisis.

When I was in my 20s, I didn't have a good grasp on how to

cope with stress, relationships, finances, or trauma from my past. My stress level was out of control and I was struggling with severe constipation, a common symptom of stress and anxiety. Although I worked as massage therapist, a health field aimed at relieving stress and improving a sense of wellbeing for others, I felt utterly disconnected from my own body. I took my work seriously and I derived comfort and enjoyment through my work when I was able to relieve my client's pain. My hands and fingers were invested all day in the searching for knots and trigger points in muscles, moving energy through meridians, waiting for the eventual heave and sigh of breath that signaled my client was finally relaxed and at ease.

In nearly 10 years of investing myself in the wellbeing of others through massage and bodywork, I had not invested much in my own wellbeing. Although I was lean and appeared fit, my well was running dry and my health was declining. Eventually, it came to the point where I could not even read my body's signals of thirst which resulted in dehydration, nor satiation after eating. My irregular eating habits and lack of proper nourishment were slowly causing an intestinal blockage. One time I had to take myself to the ER for severe abdominal pain due to constipation, which a doctor pointed out to me on my X-ray with a smirk on his face. Of course this was something that could have easily been prevented with a little extra fiber and prune juice, precisely what was prescribed to me upon leaving the ER. I remember feeling embarrassed by my lack of body-awareness, but resolved to never let it happen again, which it did a year later. I'm not one who learns from the first time walking into a wall. I suffered that one alone in the bathroom until the episode passed.

In addition to the disconnection I felt from my body, I also suffered with strained personal relationships. Being a strong-willed person, I did a lot of adulting on my own and rarely took good advice, which eventually earned me a gut full of guilt and shame for poor choices I had made for myself. To make me feel a little better I surrounded myself with needy, manipulative individuals who were worse off than me, thereby marginally increasing my self-worth. I backlogged my stress and carried my burdens with a martyr's pride. I had a lot of forgiving and releasing to do, but that took more time than I wanted to give and more feeling of my feelings than I wanted to experience, so I spent a lot of my daily energy shoring up the dam of emotion and backlogging spiritual information that I had been suppressing for many years. I lived in my head trying to reason my way out of feeling my feelings, or distracting myself with endless activity followed by exhaustion. Luckily, I was spared access to drugs and the lack of serious motivation to locate them, or this very well could have been my story about awakening through addiction and sobriety.

One of my primary teachers and colleagues who knew me well suggested that I try yoga so that I could keep my body stronger and my mind more stable, at least to prolong my massage career. If I took some yoga classes and found that it suited me, perhaps I should learn to teach and split my time between the two until I could decide what I wanted my future to look like. After just a few classes, I had determined that the physical component of yoga made perfect sense and that I must pursue it diligently. I observed many of the same anatomical and energetic principles in the physical practice of yoga that I had acquired in massage and bodywork such as human anatomy, alignment, and posture. It was a perfect fit.

Although other forms of yoga were available in my area at the time, hatha yoga is where I started because it was movement-based which perfectly suited my highly distractible and agitated mind. But then something almost magical happened at the end of the class. It was a vigorous hatha yoga class, possibly even inappropriately challenging, because I didn't know how to do anything with moderation. In the quiet of the post-practice meditation I dropped into a peaceful stillness that I hadn't felt since I was child. I noticed my body felt very heavy but completely comfortable, and my mind was calm. I longed to have more of these experiences, and I sought to one day soon be able to afford proper training in yoga and meditation.

As a single parent with limited means and a tight schedule, I got frustrated and tired often. When I tried replicating the experience of the yoga class when I was at home, nothing short of a cage of monkeys, a herd of elephants, and ten movie screens were all going on in my head at the same time! For months, not a single moment of inner peace could be extracted from the whole burning heap, not one single moment of clarity grappled to stand out from the rest. In between private pity-parties and self-loathing, I would try to make it up to myself by sneaking in some of what I could remember of the yoga classes.

I would light a candle, put on some bass-thumping electronica music to drown out the voices in my head, and have a yoga-dance party all to myself. I attempted to simulate what I experienced in yoga class, but I had nearly zero experience in yoga and dance, so what actually came out of me was explosive creative movement. I made a good therapy session of it in my second-floor apartment, and I took advantage with the noise level for my downstairs neighbors were all deaf. I followed my body's desire to reach and stretch, twirl like a dervish, and throw my head around like a metalhead at a head-bangers ball! When I was tired, I laid down.

This weekly yoga-dance got me good and tired much like a strong hatha yoga class, and then I was able to settle down and "peace out." Then the second Spiritual Awakening occurred in my life. One day, slowly, out from the mental fog, emotional and spiritual messages came churning out which had been pent up all those years. Hidden from my consciousness for decades, I had repressed them with my incessant drama, frequent moving, stressful living conditions, and high maintenance relationships. When I was finally ready to listen to myself and to the Universe, my "yoga-dance" had cracked the lid open from a steaming pot of unprocessed feelings and spiritual information.

When clarity came, I received a Gift from Spirit. I was reminded

THE GIFT OF AWAKENING

of my first Spiritual Awakening and the reason I am here in this body. I was reminded of my past life, my connection to the web of All That Is, and what my work on Earth should be. I felt clearly that I must not delay gaining more knowledge about health and wellness, if only to attend to my own health, and that the knowledge gained from that effort would guide me on. At that moment, I was not yet ready and able to sit down quietly and listen to everything the Universe had to say, but I got the message loud and clear that one day soon I would have to. I chose not to deny myself forgiveness, growth, clarity, and expansion any longer.

I believe that the events that led to this awakening could be considered the result of a barely-contained crisis of imbalanced and erratic energy in my mind and body. By normalizing erratic or imbalanced energy, it is possible to not only survive a spiritual crisis, but also thrive from its lessons and come to see it as a gift. Yoga is certainly not the only way to balance energy, but the movement and deep breathing followed by stillness and contemplation is indeed the pathway I took. I am certain that merely stretching and twisting into postures at that pivotal time would not have had the same positive result that yoga, movement, and mindfulness did for me. Stiff bodies gradually getting more limber as one would do calisthenics or stretches simply do not remove all the obstacles to stuck energy. It helps, but it's not the full story. Twisting oneself into a pretzel shape as seen in social media images purporting to be yoga, likewise do not create the circumstances of unifying your soul with the Divine. Over the years, I have discovered that an effective self-care practice includes movement, mindfulness, a clean diet and time in nature will help gently awaken spiritual gifts that can either lead one out of a crisis or help prevent one from occurring. It is possible that if I had known about yoga earlier in life, I may have followed an easier life-path, but I'll never know. I prefer to think that it was all leading me to be more compassionate. Perhaps my suffering, crisis, and awakenings led me to seek the education I needed to find my teachers and my tribe.

– 26 –

Awakening from Sorrow & Grief

INFANT SOUL

The creator holds space in
Infinite space and time
Waiting like an hourglass with no sand
or pendulum hanging still.
Your tiny heartbeat, felt without yet a sound
of thrum, swish, swash
tumbling about
in the warm wash of the womb
of the universe
My evolving infant soul—
When will you emerge?

Sorrow can arise as painful truths that open the heart of compassion. The Gate of Suffering is one pathway to awakening we wish would never happen. We wouldn't wish the sadness, grief, loss, and despair on anyone, yet it happens to nearly every one of us, and it is an opportunity to accept some universal truths of existence in human form. The Gate of Sorrow is a dark and sad life experience that eclipses the mundane world, like a brush with mortality and death. But when we grieve and receive healing from the event, suddenly or over time, it can result in a positive and permanent Spiritual Awakening that is of immense benefit. Awakening through this gate, you will have walked through the fire and not only lived to tell about it, but learned that you and your suffering are not the same. The ultimate lessons learned from passing through the Gate of Suffering are releasing mental and emotional attachment from anything you cannot control, and accepting the truths of change, disappointment, and death.

Nearly every great spiritual master and teacher has experienced great pain, loss, or tragedy that caused a positive shift in awareness; however, many people are unable to make the transition and remain defeated and paralyzed by suffering. Easier said than done, but there are healing practices that will assist you in getting free from grief and suffering. Just making the best out of a really sad or painful situation is not the same as emerging from suffering, so some internal work and healing must be done. Emerging from suffering with a gift takes a combination of a few special circumstances: the courage to face sorrow with awareness, receiving adequate validation and support from others, and receiving (or taking) sufficient time for healing. Awareness, support, and healing time are the three jewels that sit atop the golden arch of the Gate of Awakening through Sorrow.

I arrived at the Gate of Sorrow having already gone through the Sacred Gate of Oneness earlier in life which, by contrast, was not one bit physically painful or uncomfortable at all. I experienced the greatest amount of sorrow in my life the year that my eldest son moved away from home. This may not seem nearly as bad as someone else's sorrow involving the death of a loved one, but there was a death in my life: the death of my identity. I was a single parent for many years before I married, and my child was everything to me. My identity and sense of purpose was embedded in my role as a single mother which had created an inflated sense of pride in raising him mainly on my own, and so when the time came for him to leave me to go live with his father, I felt devastated and abandoned and my sense of identity fell apart. I also felt guilt that I should have done more to preserve his contentment with me, and fear that letting him go was sending my beloved child to walk into the mouth of a great beast and possibly lose him forever. Fear, guilt, and loss of identity were all wrapped up in this sorrowful package. I am happy to say that my son is alive and well and our relationship has improved greatly, but at the time I had no hope that there could be any benefit to this situation for either of us.

Many people experience this kind of sorrow when their child moves away to college or gets married, often called "empty nest syndrome," because it is characterized by emotional upsets that affect all areas of our life. For me, the paradox of my grieving state is that I wasn't even alone: I had my husband and my four-year old son at home for whom I needed to remain a stable, loving parent. I also struggled with a compounded grief and loss for my younger son's feeling of abandonment by his older brother.

I felt emptied of this defining role I played in life, which left me utterly without an identity. I had entered a black hole in my emotional space, and could not pull myself out for the better part of a year. I had faith that my yoga and meditation practice would help me, and I intellectually knew that 'this too shall pass' as all grief does when properly processed. However, during every single unoccupied moment I experienced deep, dark, sadness for a long time.

This was my Sacred Gate of Sorrow—with a capital S. I was unaware at the time that I was experiencing a life-changing lesson to essentially unlearn what society taught me about who I think I am. I was originally a 'Single Mother', but I felt I was a 'Good Mother', which I valued more than almost anything else in this world. You can just hear the capitalization of the word when people own a role, whether in pride or shame over their identity, marital status, career, or nationality such as, "I'm Divorced," "I'm a Confirmed Bachelor," "I'm a Lawyer," or "I'm an American." The labels placed on us by society or those we place on ourselves are destructive when we cannot see who we are without them.

I clung to and craved my identity as a Mother because it placed me securely within the story of my life where I knew my role well. I was young when my son was born so this was one of the first major roles in my life to give me purpose and perspective. I had not yet become anything else in the world. My self-identity as an independent single mom was a great source of personal pride and my basis for relating to the world. I had no idea being a Mother would turn out to be a dysfunctional self-identity until it was being scraped away. Although I had been practicing meditation and yoga for many years beforehand, no one could have foretold to me that this one relationship, this one person, this one child, could shake my world to the ground. The physical absence of my son, my counterpart as a Mother, peeled apart the layers of my self-identity into a fragile and raw state.

Over the course of a year, I received emotional support and movement therapy to move through the entire well-published Elisabeth Kubler-Ross's *Stages of Grief*: denial, anger, bargaining, depression, and finally into acceptance. I feel the process of moving through the stages were the three jewels on the gate: I accepted the reality of the situation that my son was not going to change his mind, I allowed myself support and love from my husband and friends, and I spent time every day to meditate, cry, and journal my feelings. I did a metta meditation which focuses on lovingkindness toward my son to extend well-wishes of love and compassion, despite how sad and hurt I felt. The antidote to my sadness was love. Sometimes I was praying through my tears, but one day I realized I could just send love and I was no longer sad.

Sometime later that year, I reread Jack Kornfield's book with descriptions of the Gates of Awakening, quite certain that I had moved through the Gate of Sorrow. I gradually began to feel relieved that this kind of deep suffering may actually never need to happen again in my life! I had learned an epic lesson in detachment in the presence of unconditional love, and I was able to determine healthy boundaries for my expression of grief through awareness, support, and healing time. From that point on, I decided to face all of my important relationships with lovingkindness and a healthy sense of detachment, so that when my vision of a relationship is not realized, or changes, or disintegrates, I will still have my head on my shoulders and my heart intact.

When I was in the middle of it, I had no idea when it might end, but I had faith that I would come to understand why I was emotionally drowning. Moving through this Sacred Gate of Awakening, I was able to discern how my suffering was directly linked to my attachment of the actions of another person. Now, you might expect that a year of suffering would teach me never to love again!

Or that suffering is the only way to live when you feel abandoned by someone you love. Or that denial is the best strategy for pushing painful emotions away. But, no. A year of suffering with pure awareness of the process was what it took to teach myself how to handle loss and grief for the rest of my life.

I suppose I could give you heart-wrenching detail why this particular person was so special to me, why I couldn't just enjoy having some extra time on my hands and extra space in my house, or why I felt that my son defined me as a human being, but that would be quite unnecessary. The fact is that most people feel defined by things that are not truly them, such as career, marital status, parental status, family role, gender, and so forth. Unless you've already given up your earthly identity, we should not judge one another's suffering because it is specific to each individual. What *is* important is to know what *you* think identifies you, because it is precisely those things that will rock your world when they suddenly change! It is what you don't know about your mind that will trip you up and leave you spinning right down to the ground. I used this experience to walk through the Sacred Gate of Suffering, so now I can see it as a wonderful gift.

Just going through suffering, as everyone does at some time or another, does not mean you've had a spiritual awakening, or everyone would be wide awake right now and there would be peace on Earth. The problem is how we identify ourselves with suffering and loss, as I did for the better part of that momentous year. Prolonged suffering is one way to make one sick, destroy important relationships, and create even more suffering in the world. I'm not saying that the road through the Gate of Awakening through Suffering is paved with a lifetime of martyrdom or that having one awakening will solve all of life's problems. It's a lifetime journey, which is also a healing journey, but it's more rewarding and helpful for others if one chooses to be on this journey. Encounters with the Sacred Gate of Awakening through Suffering provides a precious opportunity to learn about the human condition and to generate greater compassion for yourself and others who have experienced grief and loss.

How will you know when you've moved through the Sacred Gate of Suffering? The lesson is learned when you realize you are *not* the labels you identify with. You are not your suffering or other aspects of your human life like your relationships or your work. Approval doesn't define you any more than suffering does. You are not a name that is given to the roles you play in life. The feelings of loss and anxiety come from an attachment to what you think you have, especially that of life and death. When those attachments fade, you may feel prompted to remember who you are created to be, or pursue a call to action that reflects a higher purpose. When you have peace and have learned a great lesson, you will have moved through the Gate of Suffering.

The gift of the Sacred Gate of Suffering is the realization that labels, names and feelings do not define us and are not part of our uniquely individual DNA. When threatened with the potential loss of our own life, someone close, or something else important, healing begins by meditating on releasing the attachment with love. It is liberating to realize that life is precious and fleeting and when faced with tragedy, meditation can help begin healing. This is not a one-time magic trick or a Band-Aid for grief; healing meditation is something you can do daily that will gradually empower you to feel whole and complete. You can eventually heal your grief by opening yourself to the feeling of freedom that comes from letting go of people or things you cannot keep. When you have made the choice to heal from suffering, you can anticipate a gift from awakening.

4

THE BEACH BUM-SCRUFFY MINISTER

ROUGH PATH

Withered, dried, dead petals lay behind me
Paths of gravel, stone, grass, and broken glass
Leading in all directions.
Though I know enough of the pleasures and pleadings from pain
To stop me in my tracks,
I will walk ahead bleeding from the soles of my feet,
And smell each of the roses in this fragrant garden along the way.

My earliest memories are filled with adventures in non-conformity with big plans for doing things someone else didn't want me to do. Boundaries did not hold much meaning for me and I was not caught nor disciplined often enough to sufficiently discourage me from minding the business of others or entering restricted areas. I lacked healthy boundaries and was abundant in curiosity. As a precocious child and teenager, I studied and challenged my closest relationships and later on created or allowed intimacy by testing the limits of trust and disclosure. The particular interest with which other people interfered in my exploration was the degree to which I held close my secret encounters.

It didn't occur to me at the time that there might be a good reason why someone should have boundaries. I yearned to explore and understand the world through the study of cause and effect, which for me was the study of how people came to be the way they are and in the situations in which they found themselves. Seemingly random encounters with strangers would end up at a 24-hour coffee shop long into the night, or a stroll down to the beach to talk out deep thoughts. My independent free-spirit attitude and lack of supervision led me to few misfortunate events, but I consider myself extremely lucky to have met Divine connections in human form.

One summer vacation when I was 15, I took a solo field trip by bicycle to the beach several miles away from my home. I planned my excursion that morning over breakfast, told no one about it, and rode my bikinied butt down to the beach with only the bare necessities: $20 and a beach towel. I arrived at the beach with no incident and found a nice space in a clearing on the sand to lay my towel down. I lay on the hot sand for a little while, then turned over and sat up to watch the waves and noticed a scraggly, possibly homeless, middle-aged man about a hundred feet away casually watching me. One might worry that this unattended young girl would be preyed upon by a man at the beach, but fearlessly I smiled and he smiled back. Although there were other people around that day, there was no one between us, and it took only a few minutes for him to make his way over to me. This situation could have gone bad really quickly but I had never spoken directly to a "beach bum" before and I wanted to know all about his life.

Several hours passed with this angel who showed great compassion for me. Thirty years later, I don't recall having learned anything about the life of the "beach bum" at all. My deliberate attempt to interview the man was gently turned around on me and I realized that it was his intent to bear witness to my thoughts and concerns and to help me understand things more clearly. He asked some poignant questions to help me work through my own teenage conflicts of school, work, and family, which he listened to with great care, attention, and respect. I shared about my how my parents had divorced and my mother was married to an abusive man. I was at the beach because I recently came to live with my dad and he was at work. I had left my mother's house to escape the abuse but was torn about leaving to start a new life at a new school. I deeply missed my friends and my precious brother who stayed behind at our mother's house. I worried about him constantly and could do nothing to save him or convince him that he would be better off moving with me. I had many valid reasons for being upset but as any parent of a teenager knows, there are many distorted views caught up in the reality of life.

The beach bum image in front of me transformed into a scruffy minister. The man carried a great spirit with him. Every memory I have of this encounter was indeed spiritual but not dogmatic and he made no attempt to convert me to any religion. He was kind and patient and seemed to absorb any negativity right out of thin air. He did not waste energy arguing with a teenage girl about why she should be grateful for her life and be more patient in the process of growing up, nor did he commiserate with me. Every negative thought I voiced to him was reframed or redirected so that I could see clearly where I had made a right choice, and that it was my limited view of circumstances that created more of a problem for myself. He encouraged me to gain wisdom over time, and assured me that my views would change and I would feel better. Instead of trying to solve my problems, or distort them further by putting me in my place, he was the spotless mirror to see my own mind crystal clear.

I got a glimpse of enlightenment that day, and I knew that everything in my thoughts and emotions were temporary. I knew they would change over the course of many lifetimes and therefore I should not be attached to any one way of seeing things. Out of nowhere I remembered the enlightened moment in my room when I was 6 years old and I told him about it in a fantastically awkward and limited way which I felt he understood, just as though he had had the good fortune to have experienced a similar phenomenon as well. His validation of my experience was a gift that boosted my self-esteem in a way that had never occurred to me before. This was the first time in my life I was truly seen, heard and felt understood on a spiritual level.

My views and perceptions were changing right there in front of my eyes when I suddenly realized that the beach bum-turned-scruffy minister was glowing in light that did not come from the sun, nor any reflection from water, sand, or artificial source. This was a light that did not hurt my eyes and it gave me comfort and peace. The conversation came to stillness and there were no words. I allowed myself to sit quietly a minute taking it all in and he was as patient as though he was waiting for me to start the conversation again at my own readiness. But then a momentary doubt of my senses turned to sincere concern for the man whom I thought might be feeling strange and hot from this intense light! His expression nor posture changed at all and I thought he must not know what I saw but he made no indication that he was bothered at all.

And then everything changed. My eyes averted to the horizon. I nearly panicked when I realized that the sun was going down and I still had several miles to ride on my bicycle to get home on time for dinner. When I stood up to part ways with the man, he remained seated. I felt awkward and a little embarrassed when I realized my view had shifted back to seeing the man as a beach bum in all his scruffiness. In my hurry to get back home, I hastily packed up and took my leave. I could not see his light anymore and I did not know how to properly thank him because I was unsure what had happened and where the day went. I was all too aware of his dirty, ragged appearance again and I was confused that I couldn't see him any longer as the angel I saw only a moment ago. I was disconnected again from spirit in the material world. I got back on my bike and rode away from the sunset. I cannot recall how I even said goodbye.

When I assured my father at dinner that night about my remarkable day at the beach, I struggled to share about my encounter with a strange man. To my family's shock and bewilderment, my initial description of the man related more to his physical appearance. Describing the spiritual aspect of how his appearance changed over the following hours did nothing to comfort my parents, so I resigned to assuring them of my safety and I never spoke of it again.

5

Deliberate Awakening

Emboldened by the thin light
She strained for more
Until her mold shattered,
Releasing her exuberantly.
Floating now on high,
Shimmering in the sun,
She scorns the earth.
Will she see, one day,
That the light is also here,
Illuminating the earth,
Her children, friends, and lovers,
The here and now?

~Anonymous
(Poem from *The Stormy Search for the Self*, by Stanislav Grof)

I have had spontaneous, sudden awakenings and also deliberate awakenings followed by crises, followed by more awakenings marking the stages of my life like milestones. One might wonder how this kind of thing could happen to someone over and over again, or why on Earth someone would ever try to deliberately bring it upon themselves? Spiritual seekers and thrill seekers alike run with burning desires to glimpse the Light of their Creator. And nothing brings people closer to God than death or the fear of it; therefore, putting oneself in an intensely dangerous, or fearful position are some of the conditions that can precede a peak experience as a powerful catalyst toward enlightenment. If you are eager and resilient for living through the consequences of dramatic actions, it may seem worth the risk, but positive outcomes can never be guaranteed.

There is a certain measure of wisdom that can be gained through suffering by leading a chaotic and undirected life, or even a tightly controlled one. Grasping conditions too tightly or too loosely is how people end up co-creating the conditions for suffering as a way to learn about energy in the most effective, yet unpleasant way. Whether ingesting dangerous substances, or pushing the body beyond its natural limits, spiritual awakening should not be induced at the risk of having a crisis.

I personally needed to experience a disconnection from the Divine and suffer with my health for awhile to understand why being in connection was a better choice. If I am really honest with myself, I can see how the circumstances for spiritual awakening developed in a serendipitous way with some credit given to my insatiable curiosity, and the rest to good teachers and Divine guidance. I do not blame anyone else for causing me to suffer temporarily so that I could acquire the experiences I needed to awaken. Any disconnection I have had in my mind-body-spirit was mostly due to my ignorance or resistance of Divine guidance. Riding miles to the beach with no supervision, companion, or a cellphone (there were no cellphones in the 1980s) to sit with a strange person who could have done me great harm is an example of Divine grace. I feel it was my deliberate seeking that brought the appropriate experience that caused awakening, but in seeking there is always the possibility of finding catastrophe.

If you've had a spontaneous awakening that created any kind of crisis with a long recovery period, you may hardly be able to imagine that some folks covet what you have and seek to achieve that peak experience by any means necessary. It may sound enticing and exotic to experience the sacred rituals of spiritual awakening, but be warned that the intentional induction of altered states can cause more harm than good when used at the wrong time through the wrong methods, or improperly supervised. An attempt to deliberately alter one's reality with long exposures to physical or mental stress or pain, perceived or actual life-threatening situations, or psychoactive plant usage can be dangerous madness.

Every culture in every country of the world has accepted methods toward achieving a supra-ordinary state of consciousness. Mystics and monks, spiritualists and shamans, musicians, artists, and visionaries—everywhere in the world throughout history people have found ways of attaining a state of consciousness that transcends normal mental activity which brings about higher creativity, productivity, and a sense of unity. Unusual experiences are not uncommon during the widely accepted Eastern practices of Zen meditation, Kundalini yoga, martial arts, and chi gong, but natural mind-altering medicinals such as cannabis are gaining acceptance as well. The Native American tradition of smudging and smoking a blend of herbs, called kinnikinnick, were believed to heighten awareness and connect with nature's highest wisdom. Native Americans believed that plants had life and power, and that taking them into the body under the right circumstances and with the right intent were a part of the spiritual quest.

Some religions include fasting, or the restriction of food, as a method of depriving the body into a state of higher awareness. Natural or drug-induced sleep deprivation can cause supra-normal states of consciousness for creativity and feelings of euphoria. Alternately, just as often the opposite effect can occur such as depression and delusion. The problem with fasting, sleep deprivation, or any type of asceticism is that the body sees deprivation as a state of emergency and depletion.

For example, deprivation from short term fasting is usually not a problem for a healthy adult. The problem occurs the next day when the person is in a lousy mood with a stomach upset resulting from binge-eating. The Western methods of enhancing the mind–spirit connection tend to be more pharmaceutical than herbal, but either approach can bring upon a crisis or emergency that persists for hours or days, with the real possibility of doing permanent damage.

Spontaneous awakening isn't usually a choice, but I am convinced that gradual awakening with support and healing time is a more desirable experience. Wouldn't you rather come out of a dream with a back rub rather than a cup of ice water thrown in your face? It is not uncommon for unusually blissful or mystical states to occur in people engaging in specialized breathing and energy practices such as Kundalini yoga or holotropic breathwork which is a type of hyperventilation breathing technique. Likewise it is not uncommon for spontaneous awakening to occur through a daydream, nightdream, a deep connection with nature, intense love-making, or prolonged seated meditation.

Regardless of the method to achieve a peak experience, you need to give yourself time to recover or both your day to day functioning and your health will eventually and dramatically decline. Problems arise when energy bubbles up to the surface of your consciousness too soon or too fast from beneath a blockage with accumulated, unprocessed emotional, sensory, or spiritual information. The decision to deliberately bring about awakening through the intake of a substance such as smoke, herb, pill, drink, etc. or even deliberately bringing yourself into circumstances that will dramatically alter your perception is throwing open the gates to new information and sensation to enter you. At some point the human container must process or digest this new information. As I mentioned before, I could hardly describe what was occurring to me for two important reasons: my limited vocabulary in describing spiritual exchanges— and also that I had not allowed enough time to rest and process the encounter. When you bring upon a heightened experience in unfamiliar surroundings or with unfamiliar methods, you open the door to a whole load of new information that your body and mind have to process.

Another time I was introduced to LSD and got lucky in my experiment with expanding my consciousness while a friend was not so lucky. I wanted to have the experience because I thought I liked to live dangerously, but I had enough caution and insecurity that I wanted somewhat controlled conditions. I at least wanted someone who cared about me to make sure that I would be alright and stay around to take care of me if something went badly. I had heard from friends and read in books that one could have either tremendous euphoria with an explosion of creativity or spiritual insight or go completely insane even from the first time taking the drug. That was intriguing information. I was reassured by my friends that they would look after me, so I was ready to cautiously try it for a deliberately heightened experience.

I tore off a tiny corner of the white piece of LSD infused paper provided to me and waited anxiously for something to happen. A half-hour later, colors bloomed vividly, walls began to breathe, and my heart swelled with love. When I lay still on the floor the experience was similar to the mindful awakening I had when I was six, but with additional hypnotic visual hallucinations that lasted for a full eight hours. Thankfully, I experienced no visits from dead people. I did, however, write poetry and sang songs and expressed, in a somewhat limited way, my philosophy about how everything is connected. In my mind, we were All One.

On that very same night, another friend of mine who also had never tried LSD decided that he wanted to go big and completely lose his mind. His determination to have a big spiritual experience was a near tragedy. He had stupidly consumed a whole hit of the drug in one night and ended up crying in the bathroom most of the night hiding from paranoid delusions of space aliens and was in no position to be of any help. Quite selfishly I didn't want him to bust my groove because I was in a really interesting and delight-ful state of mind. I stayed by my sober friend the whole night and woke up feeling dehydrated and hungry, but otherwise fine. This is a good example of one person feeling enlightened as a result of an experience and the other feeling traumatized in a crisis. In the span of a few years that followed, I took the drug about 10 different times, but once I learned to meditate I was able to create a similar experience of Oneness by just breathing and focusing my mind. From that point on, I never desired to get high through artificial means ever again.

It is my understanding through years of practice with breathing that no permanent damage has ever been done to the body and mind by increasing energy through simply breathing the air. No matter how deeply you breathe, how long you hold your breath, or how long you exhale, the body has an amazing capacity to regulate its levels of oxygen and carbon dioxide in the brain. If you were to hold your breath for a whole minute, or until you turn blue in the face, you would eventually pass out, lose consciousness, and start breathing again. Breathing for higher awareness requires that you stay conscious or the technique doesn't work. The results of breath awareness and over-oxygenating the body produce time-limited effects, which I recommend for a gentle awakening with none of the negative side effects of hallucinogens. Therefore, I cannot recommend any of the former methods for achieving higher consciousness. I recommend mindful breathing for managing energy and expanding consciousness naturally. Breathing is an anchor to the present moment so it is one of the most practical ways to become more mindful and it costs nothing to do it. When I meet with a client or student for the first time, I always assess their breathing and guide them towards breathing with depth and ease. It is the first step to put one in a favorable state of mind for a gradual, gentle awakening. Deep breathing will naturally clear obstacles to energy flow and will increase the sensation of energy in the body and mind. Some common sensations of deep breathing practice are light-headedness, sparkles or lights behind the eyes, warmth in the body (not necessarily recordable on a thermometer), and tingles or little pulses of energy in the hands, feet, chest, or belly. Give yourself 10-30 minutes to fully experience your breathing with no other distractions.

Awakening with Breath

1. *Breath sensation.* Sit still and close your eyes. For a minute or two, feel the sensation of cool air coming into the nose and the warm air going out. Make your breathing the most important thing for the time being. Next, pay attention to the feeling of breathing in your chest. The ribs raise when you breathe in, and rest and recoil slightly when you breathe out. The rib cage moves in all directions when you breathe, not just in the front; so notice sensations in the rib cage when you breathe in underneath your arms and in your back. With your mind, pay close attention to the rise and fall of your ribs as you breathe. Feel free to yawn if you feel the impulse. After a few minutes of breath sensation, breathe naturally with no expectations. Pause in stillness before doing the next breath exercise, or before going about your daily activities.

2. *Increase your energy.* Inhaling generates energy, also known as prana. If you're feeling sleepy or dull in the mind, you may want to increase your energy naturally. Breathe in full and deep and exhale normally. For an added boost, raise your arms up over your head or even rest them on the top of your head or support them with a wall or chair. Raising the arms with full and slow breathing will gradually increase your energy and alertness.

3. *Decrease your energy.* If you have a lot of erratic energy or are feeling anxious, your breathing will likely be shallow, rapid, or held up high in the chest. If you feel anxious and want to slow down, focus on your exhalations. If it is difficult to exhale thoroughly while sitting, lay on your belly on the floor. A firm surface is necessary to slow down your inhalations and make long and slow exhalations easier and more complete. Observe

the pause at the end of your exhale. When your breathing returns to normal, return to sitting as a patient observer of your entire being. Resume with your daily activities when the time feels right for you. If your level of anxiety or nervousness increases during stillness, try an activity that encourages you to fully expend that energy such as hatha yoga, moderate exercise, or dance before you practice mindful breathing.

AWAKENING TO EMPTINESS

Mountain
Immoveable, insurmountable matter.

Then there is no mountain,
space instead
as if the mountain were never there.

Then there is a mountain
I noticed clear as day,
made of dirt and rock
and the crushing foundation of a millennia,
hours, days, and moments.

Mere minutes I have been here
sitting at the cushion
gazing at the ground
and the horizon
at the eternal sunrise and sunset
of my life.

The concept of emptiness comes from a Buddhist teaching that says all matter is empty, or void, of the qualities that we assign to it. Things are what they are and not really the stories or names or associated judgements we were taught or conditioned to assign to a thing. Saying something is empty does not mean that something does not exist; it means that what we see is made up of other things we cannot see and so we call it "empty" of the qualities we would typically use in our language to describe a thing. This realization that everything we see is "empty," can make one laugh or cry out loud at the absurdity of what we make things out to be when they are simply not. What we see, think, and feel are human mental projections—memories, impressions, associations, and feelings—that are not the actual thing themselves.

Humans are intelligent but we love our stories, images and fantasies. Most of our entertainment sources are born of our desire to tell stories and make connections no matter whether they are true or false. Human beings are constantly moving, creating and communicating endless signals to the emotional and physical body which sensationalize almost everything and anything. Realizing the nature of emptiness and it's opposite—delusion—is the beginning of unravelling every story you've ever been told about who you are in this life. A key element in meditation is to remove judgement and delusion from the mind to realize how things truly are: nothing is as it appears. Once it is realized, nothing can ever be the same again.

I was studying Buddhist philosophy for a few years when I gave myself diligently to the daily practice of meditation on the Perfection of the Heart of Wisdom sutra, which I paraphrase as "everything is nothing and nothing is everything." It sounds crazy and nonsensical, but nearly everything sounds crazy until you understand it, but as sure as the sky is blue, millions of Buddhist monks swear by its truthfulness. After three months of daily meditation and reading everything I could get my hands on about the possibility that everything in the world is "empty," a smile came to my face out of nowhere when it dawned on me that I felt I understood this implausible concept. I had cut through a great deal of my delusion that day in astonishment followed by a belly laugh and giggles when I had a moment to myself. It was crazy and nonsensical, but real, and totally necessary for my spiritual development to detach from anything that limited me to a label or definition.

The great Buddhist teacher Shunryu Suzuki called it "beginner's mind" to have clarity of the pure nature of the mind before anything was impressed onto it. Like a newborn baby seeing the world for the first time, the mind was initially empty of claims on language and judgement until an impression was made. Although it is necessary for human survival to seek nourishment, to crave protection and love, and to discern between safety and harm, but too many words can clutter our peace of mind. With consistent practice, the beginner's mind can successfully override human conditioning with brilliant clarity. Awakening to emptiness is healing and liberating because you can easily slough off labels, unnecessary judgements, and be less reactive to others' judgements.

It is a comic absurdity that we can analyze, describe, judge and criticize something that doesn't contain a single permanent quality. In our relatively short lives, we take the creative and intellectual liberties of giving and taking names and labels to live up to, creating an identity, shaping ourselves around familial and societal obligations and call it our reality. The names and ideas we form around a thing are all mental formations, not really the thing itself.

As an example, a flower is the name we call a non-animal thing that grows in the ground with parts like stem, petals and pollen, but it is actually empty of any of the describable qualities we might assign to it: full, pink, beautiful, aromatic. Every adjective we could use to describe the rose is not actually in the rose; it is in our perception of the rose. A rose is actually just a sum of the parts that comprise what we call the rose: a stem, thorns, petals, pollen, aroma, and descriptors we use to differentiate it from other flowers. And when its stem loses moisture, the petals fall off and it dies; the non-rose parts become a part of the earth from where they arose. From this point of view, the rose is a temporary, even fleeting, identity which does not actually contain any of the qualities assigned to it. Humans have appreciation for things they see, and so we can admire the flower for what it is, but a clear mind knows it is empty of any quality. Don't attach yourself to what you see, because moment by moment the thing we appreciate is always in a state of becoming something else.

Before anyone ever called a flower a 'flower,' it just existed. It grew, lived and died when its life force dwindled or was cut off. Perhaps someone noticed it during the object's lifetime and they smiled in appreciation, but it was not assessed nor judged. Labeling and analysis kill the beauty in many things. The flower does not need anyone to assign it good or bad qualities in order for it to exist or for it to grow to its full flower-ness, or to declare the rose absent after its demise.

Moving through the Gate of Emptiness is a non-dual acceptance and liberation that all things —people, animal, and other— are what they are, free from the restriction of labeling and judgement. Nothing in this life holds a continuous positive or negative evaluation. But a human is a social being and has more senses and awareness than a flower. We do care whether our 'flower-ness' is acceptable to the other flowers in our community. As a social being it is a matter of necessity to differentiate what is safe from what is harmful and to have some societal connection. But a person who spends a lot of time in meditation on the nature of the mind may experience a liberation from the labels of all things which we can call Zen, or the Gate of Awakening through Emptiness.

For someone who sees that everything is interrelated and interdependent of all other things, words are just clutter and confusion. Now, if you decide to take up an argument with your neighbor who is admiring your rose bushes and you claim they are empty and are not, in fact, rose bushes, this can be confusing and confrontational. Taking this viewpoint into the world for discussion will make you a social outcast, but if you ask a Buddhist monk, they will happily affirm your correct view and invite you to tea. You don't need to be a monk if you feel that words often get in the way and that silence is golden. Choose your interactions carefully and give yourself the quiet time you desire. Through the Gate of Emptiness is where you'll have a good chuckle at the silliness humans make for themselves with words, then you'll have the rest of your life to realize that you don't have to live by a label ever again.

6

I HAVE ALWAYS BEEN AWAKE: ARIEL'S STORY

What do people mean by the word "normal?" When I was a child, I could see Spirit Guides, read into the future, hear peoples' thoughts and sense and communicate with ghosts and other beings. My story about spiritual awakening started from a baseline of already being awake and moving forward from that point.

To me, being "normal" meant that everyone could do these things. I was aware of the non-physical aspect of reality at age three, and my abilities never stopped from that point forward. To most people, being "normal" meant that they were not aware of a non-physical world. I feel most people act like they are asleep, not using their full brains to be aware of levels of existence that, while not being a part of the Third Dimension, are still real and affect us all the time. Many people are aware of the non-physical aspect of reality at a very young age, but for some reason shut that down somewhere around age five or six.

At about age six I realized that I needed to stop talking about the "see-through people" that were my Guides and about telling the future or hearing what people were thinking. I understood that if adults realized that I knew what they were thinking, or could talk to non-physical beings, that there might be negative consequences. My next-door neighbors were very religious and I could only imagine what they might think of me.

So I began a path of research, looking for other people like myself. In the early 1970s the few books available on the auric field said things like, "If you have black in your aura, it means you are a bad person," and the conversation about ESP (extra-sensory perception) was limited at best. I began testing myself for accuracy by predicting face-down cards and by testing my ability to read thoughts with close friends. I would get an intuitive "hit" about a future event and wait to see if it would come true and it frequently did. I meditated constantly, communicated with my Guides daily and kept looking for friends on the path. My search for others like me continued for years.

My big test of initiation came when I was 12 to prove once and for all if my spiritual Guides were trustworthy. One day, I did everything my Guides told me not to and ended up with a broken wrist. For some reason, I was transported to the hospital Emergency Room and was not treated for pain for over six excruciating hours. I finally had my answer—my spiritual Guides were real and I should follow their guidance. Although I was in great pain, this realization gave me a lot of peace. Finally, I could totally trust my Guidance.

From that point forward, I worked on developing my ability to listen to and act on Guidance (and not judge myself when I had difficulty doing that, which was often the case). I worked on my abilities to read and work with energy, and eventually, how to address my abilities as an empath who is someone who can feel or read the energies of other people. I now use my abilities as am empath in my holistic healing work to create techniques and tools to help others.

I also worked on clearing negative emotions, perceptions and fears that had built up during the course of my life and also worked on my reactions to them. I went on an odyssey of studying religious history, spiritual practices, and attending retreats and workshops to address my issues. This journey started at age 20 and has continued to the present day 30 years later. I eventually worked with Guidance to create my own energywork modality called HighSelf Resonance Therapy which I have taught to thousands of students in my vocational healing school. I have worked with thousands of clients and written thousands of pages of curriculum to educate the energy-sensitive and those in healing fields. It has been quite the journey of exploration, growth, and healing! My goal was to help two million people on their personal growth path and now having trained students who carry on my work, I know I will reach that goal.

We all experience adversity in our lives and I have had more than my share of challenges. One thing I have realized from my experiences is that the Divine Consciousness is always there even if it does not appear that way at times. It is we who forget that the Divine guides us and is present with us, and occasionally initiates adversity so that we can move forward in our consciousness. Gratitude for the process has always been an important step to getting the most spiritual mileage out of any experience. Sometimes it is difficult to be grateful for those times—and that is why we most need to work on it!

One of the gifts I have received is the art of re-framing—changing our perception of what we experience with intention. We can change the way we experience reality by changing our perception of how we experience it. This paradigm shift can make even the most grueling of experiences into something uplifting and rewarding. Another gift I have received is that I built a community of people like me while on my journey. As a child, I sought a community. Now as an adult I have created safe spaces so people like me have a tribe and a place to talk about their experiences and work together. Some of them have even started businesses together or have gotten married! They found a safe harbor to express themselves and their version of "normal." It is vital for spiritually-inclined people to find their Sangha, the Buddha's term for a community of meditators, so they can practice their dharma, and walk their true path.

One of the things I am often asked is, "When does the journey of working on yourself stop?" I say, when you no longer have something to work on! Another way of looking at this is when we fully love and accept ourselves as we are—then we no longer have some fault to correct. Then we can fully be of service to others. I noticed that when I was in my late thirties my journey stopped being about fixing myself because I loved and accepted myself. Then it became more about expressing my truest Divine self consistently in the world (and not just the spiritual world). Now at the age of 50 my mission is about experiencing and expressing love. One of my spiritual teachers talked about how many people are in such a great need for love, and I agree—it is the spiritual food that feeds us all.

As my journey continues, sharing and expressing love is my dharma and is my version of "normal." I make a habit of expressing love and kindness daily toward myself, with my family and friends, and to strangers. It makes the world a better and happier place, and it gives me peace. I wish you love and peace on your journey.

7

EXTRA~SENSORY PERCEPTION

*Do you hesitate sharing your most intimate realizations with
anyone because they would dismiss you?
Or worse, that you're crazy?
How can a bird explain the wind to a fish?*

It is a precious opportunity to meet someone who has dedicated
themselves to the relief of suffering of all beings. I had the good
fortune to be introduced to a Tibetan lama by a childhood friend
and disciple of Tsori Dechen Rinpoche who had accepted my in-
vitation to give a talk at my center while he was in the Los Angeles
area. The dharma talk was held as a special fundraiser for a monastery he was building in Mainpat, India for buildings and monastic
education of Tibetan refugee orphans living in India. The man who
provided my introduction to the Buddhist monk was writing a
biography at the time about Rinpoche's life to also help raise additional funds for the new monastery. The following excerpt from
"Tulku: An Autobiography of a Bodhisattva" written by Vinay Ka-
thuria is a good example of how spiritual gifts, reincarnation, and
past-life-memory are gradually accepted in other cultures.

"Although I was only a child and had rarely left the small refugee settlement where I was born, these scenes were somehow familiar to me. I pressed up against the glass, and said to myself, "I
remember that place! I've been there! I know where that road leads.

And that house! That was my house that I gave to my disciples. And those cows are the family of the cows I gave my students!" My grandfather noticed me and smiled. He must have thought then that I was simply lost in the fantastical notions of a child. Later he and many others would come to realize that this was the first I would speak of things that were not of this lifetime.

When my mother learned of this unusual game of talking about things I couldn't possibly know, it only caused her to worry. Naturally, she wanted to protect me from anyone thinking that I was different from other children. "What will others say?" and "How will this child get along in school?" she would entreat my father. But soon I would seem to become quite skilled at this game, and I began to say things like, "Why am I here? I am a Lama. I should return to the monastery. I should return to my retreat." Mother would try to talk me out of this by saying, "No, no. You are just a small child now. You shouldn't worry about such things." But what a surprise it must have been for her when I began to predict things that would later come true!

My incredible stories soon became popular in our tiny village in the settlement, and each day my claims became more and more elaborate. By now, I was even calling myself Dubthop Tsoru Dechen Rinpoche - the name of a once great master from the region of Chamdo in Tibet. I ran around the village all day telling everyone to make preparations, and that I was going to pray for them, and that I would give them Empowerments, and that I would perform all the duties of a Lama. I was often teased and even called crazy. I couldn't understand why others didn't believe me."

Tulku Tsori Rinpoche is a spiritual teacher who was aware from a young age of his previous incarnation, Yogi Tsoru Dechen Rinpoche. Nobody believed him at first because young children naturally play and fantasize about high achievement and special powers, but it is actually not uncommon in Tibetan culture to be recognized as a tulku, a person who retains the knowledge and wisdom of a spiritual tradition from a previous life or incarnation. The young monk had a depth of wisdom and knowledge that he simply could not have acquired at his young age, but this phenomenon is not uncommon. The Tibetan Buddhist culture accepts that energy transfers from some beings into others, usually upon their death. If the individual recalls the memories of a previous life, they make efforts to verify it, and then they can be accepted by the community as a tulku. In Western society, this type of vivid recollection of historical vision, or past-life experiences, are not less common, but they are dismissed too often as fantasy, and it is difficult to verify by western standards. Unfortunately, in some cultures and religions memories of a previous lifetime is heavily doubted, and often written off as a mental delusion by adulthood.

Because of the Tibetan culture's spiritually normative belief in reincarnation, it didn't take too much convincing for the truthfulness of his claims to gain community acceptance that he was indeed a tulku, reborn as a previously deceased spiritual teacher. During the couple of times I have met the Rinpoche in person he said it was never important to him to be labeled for any prestige or personal benefit, but for the teachings to have credibility as his predecessor had done before him. With the support of his community and a world hungry for spiritual connection, he continued his education as a monk to become a well-recognized Rinpoche, or Precious Teacher, who is doing great humanitarian work bringing the teachings of Buddhist compassion all over the world.

When you have a supportive community and the words to explain how you experience things, communication gets easier between people. In smaller, conservative communities where perhaps no one ever has successfully explained a paranormal experience, language and culture are two major challenges to gaining validation in Western society. English and its Latin language counterparts are really quite limited in their ability to convey energetic or spiritual experiences, and so many attempts to share what we know and feel have fallen on critical ears. Some of the most accessible languages to spiritual and energetic experience are Chinese, Japanese, and Sanskrit, the

ancient language of India. It can be helpful to find English transla-
tions of great eastern cultural literature and texts to learn how energy
is understood across different countries and even different religious
beliefs, but we need a spiritual language of our own.

The language we use to describe what we feel is not as important when you are receiving information as when you attempt to
explain yourself to others. Until recently precious few courses in
spiritual energywork were offered, but experienced energyworkers
have developed educational and experiential classes where you can
learn how to manage energy and communicate about it effectively.

Most of the words they used were 'feeling words' the way you
would describe a sense feeling in the body—such as warm tingling,
pulsations in the hands and feet, a rush or zing of electricity up the
back, hairs lifted on the arms and neck. Most of these reactions in
the body are due to nervous system activity, as though something
had aroused their attention but with no visible stimulus. Another
common sense of energy is visual color. Sometimes it is an aura, or
colors that surround a person, and others who can "see" something
in the air that has no physical form. I even met someone who can
see colors when they hear certain kinds of music!

Some of the most commonly used words were 'sensing' and 'sensation,' 'perceiving' and 'perception,' 'feeling,' 'knowing,' and 'intuition.' All but one of these words can be attributed to the five senses
we are taught in school, sight, smell, taste, touch, and hearing, but
one cannot: intuition. One main hallmark of spiritual energy sensitivity is intuition, knowing information you were not taught, seen,
heard, or read. According to the Webster's Unabridged Dictionary,
intuition is defined as "the ability to understand something immediately, without the need for conscious reasoning" and "a thing
that one knows or considers likely from instinctive feeling rather
than conscious reasoning." The words "instinctive feeling" in this
definition required more investigation. Instinct is defined as "an
innate, typically fixed pattern of behavior in animals in response
to certain stimuli," and since every being with a brain and nervous

system has some instinct to survive, that does not explain why only a small fraction of people have intuition. The word "instinctive" here shares a connotation with the word reflex, because neither a reflex nor an instinct can be learned; reflexes and instinct are in your DNA to help you survive, such as a baby does in sucking or pulling your hand away from a hot stove. But in this definition, I doubt that intuition has much to do with instinct, because everyone has instincts, but not everyone feels that they have intuition. Intuition is a special gift that you can be born with, but it can also be repressed, something you cannot do with a reflex. You can enhance and improve intuition, but you cannot control what information is received the way you can with your other senses such as covering your ears to muffle a loud siren or closing your eyes to avoid viewing a gruesome image. Intuition is a special sense that takes time and attention to moderate your sensitivity.

I have also worked with some people who could not feel spiritual energy even after several attempts to practice chi gong, breath work, and yoga. They did experience sensations such as thermokinetic energy by the friction of rubbing their hands together vigorously and from convection when the heat from my hands was in close proximity to theirs, but they could not seem to sensitize to anything that didn't have empirical proof of its existence. Interestingly, there were a couple of things that I learned about each of the non-intuitive people that helped me to understand the obstacle to perception of subtle energy, and that was their deep commitment to a religion that clearly defined their perception of God, and a certain anxiety about clearing their mind. Even when guided to still their mind to concentrate on breathing and sensing rather than thinking, each meditation attempt was filled with prayer as they had been taught since childhood. It is my feeling that given more time to listen to God rather than talking all the time, there would be some success in developing a feeling mind to hone their intuition.

On one end of the spectrum the empath feels imbalanced

because they feel too much, while the analytical thinker is distracted from sensing. The balance between the two is the ability to moderate the flow of sense information, processing or digesting the information, and communicating their needs based on how they feel. This is one reason energy-workers and spiritual healers are working towards the development of a clear vernacular language for energy sensing and energy communication. Learning words in the physical world are based on tangible objects such as a peach that is fuzzy, soft, sweet, round, orange, and juicy and can be experienced with the eyes, hands, and mouth. Only a minuscule quantity of people can say the same about spiritual energy. Over the course of many years with steady inquiry I have made attempts to clarify energy language, most of which are modifications of sense words such as foresight and insight. The phrase "sixth sense" indicates someone has more than the standard five, but I have met many people who have far more than that! I hesitate to use the word telepathy because of its association with mind reading, which sounds intrusive, and because the Greek root word "pathos" is often connected to the word pathological. Telepathy actually means feeling or experiencing over a distance and could be one of the most accurate words to describe the ability to know something of a spiritual nature without a physical interaction. I favor the words "intuition" and "special skills" for their positive connotations with the population I work with.

When I interviewed people for their spiritual awakening stories, we talked about the different words we use to describe our special senses. Here are some of the ways they described how energy feels to them and how this information enters their consciousness:

~Tingles or pulses in the body, especially the hands and/or feet that are not derived from your own pulse or movement.

~Seeing or perceiving colors, auras, or sparkles surrounding a person, an animal, a tree, or even floating in the sky.

~Seeing faint movements in the air space not attributed to anything with physical form; an intensified visual sensation of this appears like billions of silvery particles swirling and floating around in the sky but not attributed to anything tangible in the air such as smoke or dust.

~ Goosebumps appear on the skin when truth is heard or felt. There is an association between the little hairs on the arms rising up with hearing or feeling truth, and spiritual truth in particular. It may be accompanied by warmth or tingling feeling in the body that lasts anywhere from a few seconds to a few minutes, sometimes only on one side of the body or one body part.

~Receive spiritual guidance (that we can call 'intuition') in order to avoid harm, or make better choices than we could have done without guidance. Knowing the source is not necessary to benefit from the guidance. Truth bumps or pleasing sensation often accompanies the guidance.

~Sudden emotional/mood changes that are not arising from present circumstances.

~Sudden revulsion or aversion to another person a or crowd of people that increases in intensity with proximity.

~Knowing the outcome of a situation or event prior to its occurrence.

~Receiving visits and/or communication from people who are no longer alive.

~Dreams, images, or messages that indicate a course of action or predict an event that later occurs.

Spiritual Communication

Communication begins relationships— human, animal, or spiritual— and not all relationships get off to a smooth start where everyone always understands and agrees with each other. It may take some time to realize that the universe is trying to communicate to you through senses you may not have been familiar with. Once that connection is made and you begin to trust its guidance, it is as real and meaningful a connection as some of the human bonds we share. Some people feel an emotional bond to the natural world through landscapes of rock, wind, water, and trees. Others may have a special insight into the natural world through non-verbal communication with animals, with a deep connection and compassion for their lives and their needs. Others exchange communication with disembodied entities, spirit guides and God, who have a direct effect on their day to day activities much like a trusted friend or guide. All of these are special gifts. Your relationship with Spirit can grow to benefit you and extend out to the farthest reaches of the earth, but only if you allow the time and stillness to feel it, abide in it, and listen to it.

When a dog communicates its needs through behavior, we don't question how we understood the dog. With a little time and genuine concern, we can observe their indications through our human senses and intuition that a dog is anxious, or feels sadness or pain, or has a special need. The more time we spend getting connected with an animal, we can better understand what it wants us to know to help take care of something that it cannot do itself. But if we understand that the five senses are just a human's way of sensing the world around them, a question worth asking is how does a disembodied individual or entity such as God communicate? If we were to be able to "hear" or "see" this communication, what would it be like? How can we sense this communication, and how do we interpret it? First we should acknowledge that not every communication is sent through the five senses most common to humans.

This canine-human connection bears some resemblance to spiritual communication because energy needs something or someone to move in order to accomplish something it cannot do itself, and that would be you. The dog cannot mend its own paw, but you can. There is no real mystery in how we learn to communicate with non-verbal humans and animals, yet there is still some confusion and mystery that God wants and needs to communicate with us to fulfill its purpose. If we can easily accept these connections with animals, nature, and other human beings, it seems quite reasonable to extend that acceptance to people connected to Spirit.

Spiritual communication is like the wind: it moves and affects things even though most people cannot see it. It affects everyone, though they may not understand where it comes from, how it works, or do not believe in it. But those who can perceive it and know how it works will be considered crazy— or gifted— by those who don't. Ungrounded energy can cause a person to "space out" or "zone out," which may result in being less communicative with other people for a period of time. The time spent zoning out from people is actually a "tuning-in" to Spirit. Additional time is required to process that information to decide when or if any action will follow. This time-out (or time-in, however you choose to view it) is similar to a computer slowing down or crashing, sleeping after a large meal, or the inability to speak when feeling and processing complex emotions. Zoning out is a form of meditation that is a natural response to receiving and digesting, or making sense, out of information.

Zoning out was enjoyable and a high priority to me as a child, much as meditation is a normal and regular part of my daily life as an adult. The function of that apparent non-activity was to process my extra-sensory perceptions in what I refer to now as a "cosmic download." I also did not have good control over my attention, so naturally I was directed to the most interesting thing going on which happened to be in my own head! My comprehension and completion of school assignments was a little slower than others: a report on King Tut is comparatively uninteresting to that of intuiting the emotions of my classmates or captivating visions of past lives!

Information flows between people in the form of words, facial expressions, body language, and unspoken thoughts and emotions. Some of this information you can see, some you can hear, and other parts you feel or receive through intuition. As an example of how intuition affects communication, imagine you run into a friend at the store, and he or she starts to gossip about a mutual acquaintance in a negative way. You can hear their words, their tone of voice, see their body language, and feel in your gut about whether they are telling you the truth. You could more easily understand the information and discern the truthfulness (or lack of it) because you have several sources of input, your hearing, your vision, *and* your intuition. Receiving the same verbal communication over the phone would put you at a disadvantage over hearing, seeing, *and* feeling this person in front of you. Although it may sound thoroughly awkward, but if you were to ask to hold this person's hand while they were gossiping to you, it would more than likely prohibit the gossip in the first place, simply because they have to connect to their heart by feeling you first. And when you connect to your heart, it is actually quite difficult to speak dishonestly! It may sound funny—or terrifyingly intense—but you would get the closest to the truth in any communication if you were to open all of your senses to receive it by seeing, listening, touching, and feeling all at the same time.

When the student is ready, the teacher will appear.
When the student is truly ready, the teacher will disappear.

~Lao Tsu

Unlike our common human senses, spiritual information is received with extra-sensory perception. Every relationship starts with some sort of communication, a calling out to let the other know it is there. When the conditions are right, such as a state of heightened awareness or meditation, Spirit might introduce itself, but humans can definitely reach out to Spirit as well. It takes some deep listening to get a flow of information going and most people benefit greatly from having a teacher who will support and guide you on your healing journey.

Finding a good spiritual guide or teacher is one of the most important choices you can make to fully accept how you are, that you want to care for yourself, and discover your gift. You can get a good start with books and online sources, but there is no substitute for having a teacher, someone you can talk to and receive guidance from who has traveled the path you are now on. They may be a householder or a degree holder, but a good spiritual guide does not need to wear special clothing, or have a name different from the one they were born with. They may or may not be affiliated with any religious or spiritual organization. They may or may not be a paid professional who charges a fee for their services. Most importantly they should listen to you with non-judgement, and be respectful and caring of you as an individual.

A Zen proverb advises us that, "When the student is ready, the teacher will appear," meaning that when you are really ready to have a spiritual teacher, you will have looked many places and talked to many people, that the right teacher will be available for you. When you find a teacher, do not discount the importance of you being your own best teacher—you are truly your own guru. A good spiritual teacher will help you dispel self-doubt over time by pointing you toward your own wisdom, not only by telling you what to do or think. Use discernment and common sense when choosing a teacher: do not allow a teacher to guide you to do anything that is unethical or feels wrong to you.

Here are a few guidelines when searching for a spiritual counselor or teacher.

~Observe the teacher for at least a year. Attend classes, read their statements or articles, and meet with them informally. Assess their ability to be approachable, helpful, and kind.

~ The teacher should freely provide the name of his or her teacher/s when asked.

~The teacher should serve the students' best interests.

~Ask if there is a group meeting of students. Knowing the other students will give you a good idea of how helpful the teachings are.

~Ask yourself if you are ready to accept and commit to practice.

When you have the answers to these questions, or when all of your questions about an individual have been answered to your satisfaction, only then should you accept someone to be your teacher. It may be a good idea to meet with them formally, by appointment, and let them know you have accepted them as your teacher. Not every teacher sees themselves as a teacher, but every teacher had a first student at one time, so it is possible that you could be their first formal student. In any case, finding your spiritual teacher in human form is a very important step on your healing journey.

With so much spiritual information coming through during the awakening process, communicating with human beings can get complicated. This is a major conflict of empaths and spiritually awakened people. It is natural to want to receive support from other people, but we also need some quiet. We need to make mindfulness and meditation a priority in our lives, finding a spiritual teacher or guide, and devote additional time building that relationship if we are to receive its gifts and live a life in satisfaction and wholeness. Our goal is to figure out how to use our special skills and senses for the greatest amount of good. What special skills do you have, and how might you use them to help yourself and others?

8

REGAINING MY BALANCE: SUSAN'S STORY

The undercurrent of tension had been brewing for a while. I am an emotional empath and highly sensitive person married to a critical and negative spouse. For 10 years I had learned to anticipate his moods and outbursts, and adjust my behavior, tone, and presence to avoid further conflict. My children are also highly sensitive and my youngest has autism. The stress of it all was wearing me down. I had no energy, no joy, and I was unable to focus.

One day, my husband and my mother had an incredibly explosive argument in front of me and the kids while we were undergoing an already stressful house remodel. I was in shock and felt like I was stuck in the middle with my arms being pulled in opposite directions and could not handle it anymore. That stressful incident was my rock bottom.

I took myself to a psychologist where I was diagnosed with anxiety and depression. I was prescribed anti-depressants and anti-anxiety medication from a psychiatrist which I was reluctant to take, but I felt I needed the help. In addition to regular cognitive behavior therapy, I was encouraged to do self-care, but I didn't have a clear understanding of what that would be like for me. I had long felt guilty and selfish about caring for myself, and so I hadn't for at least 10 years! At first, I tried deep breathing and mindfulness exercises, then I added going out for walks in my neighborhood, which helped little by little.

The real turning point came 10 months later when I decided to try energy healing and get back into yoga. I was lucky to find a place that offered both and it ended up being the medicine that saved me. My first reiki session was like an energetic jump-start to my system. I could feel the energy activating something inside me and I knew I needed to know more. For a few days after the first session, my body went through a cleanse where I got flu-like symptoms and my lips blistered, but I knew it would pass—and it did. It was my body's way of starting to heal.

My first yoga class was the following week and my first experience with a "sound bath" of crystal bowls resonated with me on a soul level. That afternoon I felt a euphoric high that I had never felt before. From then on, I was on a fast track of learning reiki, taking yoga and meditation classes to open my energy and awareness further.

As I regained my balance and my awareness grew, empathic and sixth-sense abilities started to flourish and it was all leading me to learn how to heal myself. A new shift in awareness had taken place and I felt like I was seeing things with the fresh eyes of a baby, in awe of just being. I had lost myself for so long and didn't know who I was, but now I had direction and passion for learning more about the healing process through reiki, crystals, vibration, and sound.

Six months from that first reiki session I was anxiety free, depression free, and off medication. I have received the gift of a new outlook on life that *we are all connected*. I know that there is still beauty in the broken things in life. I know that profound insights and lessons can always be learned from the things we experience if we just pay attention.

Looking back, I am grateful for my "rock bottom," because without it I would not be where I am now, in a season of spring! I now realize self-care is a matter of self-preservation and of the utmost priority. I learned that being a healer doesn't always mean having to DO, I can also just BE, and that in itself is healing. I still have so much to learn but the feeling of gratitude is ever present for having been gifted this new outlook on life.

9

MINDFULNESS

STILLNESS TO SILLINESS

A thought arises.
Let the thought pass.
Thought returns.
A bird chirps outside
Label the sensation 'hearing'.
Another thought.
An itch (should I scratch it?)
Label it sensation of 'touch'.
Light behind my eyes, sensation of sight.
Colors in the dark
Blue, pink, purple, red, green.
Feeling sleepy.
Breathing, sensation of breath,
in and out, sigh.
In all, this is stillness—
or is that silliness?
all mashed up between thoughts and sensations.

I'm sitting on the bed sideways now, facing a tall window.
Opening my eyes, there's this pinecone.
I slant my eyes toward the ground in front of me.

Lower, lower.
Rock, dirt, pinecone.
Finally, a place to rest my gaze
on the nook and cranny off a pointy section of a tiny pinecone.
So tiny down there on the ground
outside the window.

Stillness.
The backdrop of the ground and rock gets fuzzy
so there is nothing but the dark place off the nook and cranny
of the pinecone.
My brain creates an image, completely involuntary
from the light and dark places
of this pinecone;
a St. Bernard with its tongue hanging out
in the "face" of the pinecone.
Here, the silliness comes.
Meditation has become imagination.

Mindfulness is an act of observation of where you are and what you are doing at any given moment. Being mindful of what is going on inside of you is essential to differentiate from what is happening outside of you, knowing the difference between what is actually happening—a present moment experience—and what is not happening—imagination, memories, or delusions which are not based in reliable present moment reality. The act of being mindful is simple and virtually limitless in its application. Mindfulness does not require an altered state of consciousness nor are there any set of rules or religion to achieve that state.

Mindfulness is a natural occurrence of noticing our natural senses—one at a time—such as feeling your breathing or listening to the wind in the trees, but not trying to feel both of those at the same time. Mindfulness at the checkout line in the grocery store, we feel our feet in our shoes, toes and arches lifting, and then resting, to create more stability and ease in our posture as we wait. Taking a walk can be more enjoyable if you release attachment to the exercise component for a few minutes and be mindful of the feeling of the breeze on your skin. Prepare and eat a meal with mindfulness to thoroughly enjoy the smell and taste of each bite. Listening to a bird chirping outside your window can be the focus of hearing with mindfulness. Gazing at the horizon at sunset, or a treetop in the distance are ways to enjoy mindfulness of vision.

One of the core practices of yoga is a mindfulness of what you are doing as you are doing it so that your direction of focus is where you desire it to be. In periods of information overload, it is easy to forget that you can indeed direct your mind to slow down by paying attention to one specific sense at a time. This is why the practice of mindfulness is one of the first disciplinary and experiential practices to integrate your extra-sensory and/or spiritual gifts. If you desire to gain control over your mind and body and direct them in a positive way, you must begin with awareness of a starting point, the most convenient of which are the tools you have at hand such as your senses. If you can be patient for a little while as your mind runs in circles like an energetic child at the playground, you really are on the right road to being in control of your mind. If you notice part of your mind out of control, there is another part of your mind that can be like a loving parent who guides their young child toward their lap for rest after running around crazy at the park. The truth is that you cannot change what you are not aware of, so if you try mindfulness and you are aware of a conversation going on in your head, you will eventually be able to slow down the messages, even direct the flow of information, or stop it entirely.

Breathe in. Breathe out.
Forget this and attaining enlightenment
will be the least of your problems.

~Zen saying

Breathing is one of the clearest and most direct sensations in your body at the present moment. We use breathing as a focus in beginning mindfulness because there are infinite opportunities to tune into it and it occurs millions of times over the course of a lifetime. The average unmindful breath rate is about 16 breaths per minute, so a person who lives to 80 years of age will take more than 672 million breaths! If they anger easily or engage in strenuous activity, it is even more. According to ancient Taoist and Hindu wisdom, taking slower breaths reduces nervous system activity which contributes to longevity, such as a tortoise whose long life—up to 200 years—is said to be in part due to their breathing only four breaths per minute. Learning to slow the breath down to just five or six slow and full breaths per minute for 10–20 minutes, such as we do during breath-centered hatha yoga, can bring significant mental and physical health benefits.

Mindfulness is staying purposefully connected to the present in a nonjudgmental way. You can start by exploring your daily activities and routines so that you have an opportunity each and every day to be mindful. You don't have to change your life to be mindful, but being mindful will change your life! The most basic of ongoing, daily activity is breathing. Breathing will go on and on until your last day on Earth—and because it will continue on, with or without your active participation, it is the perfect connection to the present moment. If your desire is to feel yourself breathing as an act of mindfulness, you must work to develop the discipline to hold your attention on the act of breathing and only the related sensations of breathing: air flow around the entrance of the nostrils, a feeling of fullness across the chest and the rib cage, and a sense of softening, relaxing, or deflation when exhaling. Mindfulness is the foundation of meditation, which can lead to greater clarity, wisdom, enlightenment, and spiritual liberation. It is from that naturally calm but alert mental state that we can learn to find enjoyment in the small, mundane sensations as they arise, and experience the beauty and detachment from things as they transform, change, or die as all things do.

Breathing is the foundation of knowing what you are doing in the moment such as sitting down occupying space. This is very different from sitting down somewhere thinking of things that should've been done in the past, or fretting about something that hasn't happened. Do your best to breathe intentionally and fully such as sighing, so that it is the most prominent sensation in your body. Sighing is therapeutic and stress reducing. Do it with some audible exhalations, such as one would want to do waiting in utter boredom, or try the kind of sigh of relief and enjoyment from slipping into a warm bubble bath. Both are effective ways to breathe in an intentional way that can help drown out an endless stream of mental chatter.

If you are just beginning and notice that you cannot filter your thoughts at all, this is not too uncommon, so be kind and patient with yourself as you embrace the practice. I have found many people consider this kind of analytic mental activity to be "good planning," to be able to anticipate every possible outcome and avoid certain conditions or circumstances, but it does nothing to reduce anxiety or stress. I know for sure that humans cannot anticipate every outcome nor can we time-travel into the past to do things differently, or to say or unsay things that you feel regretful over. Practice to let things go. Sitting still to be mindful with breathing is one step toward the realization that you cannot change the past, and that only a clear mind and an open heart can give you the best possible outcome for an enjoyable future. Once you know where you are and what you are doing in the precise moment you are doing it, you can make some poignant distinctions between sensory information and spiritual information. The act of noticing the space you occupy, with no expectation or attachment to any specific outcome from sitting there in peace, provides a good foundation for an even greater depth of connection and understanding that is possible with a yoga practice.

If breathing slow makes you feel anxious or light-headed, you may not be exhaling completely and I recommend breathing while lying on your belly where the floor can assist you with more complete exhalations. Then breathe three full, smooth breaths. My general guideline is that if you can direct your attention on one thing and breathe deeply and smoothly three times in a row without losing focus, you are soon on your way to breathing four breaths with a focused mind. If you can do it for four breaths, it won't be long before you can do it for five breaths, and so on. Doing this practice every day will gradually increase the length of time of mindfulness and help significantly in the growth and awakening process. Awakening beings should not squander the opportunity daily to pause and listen and feel for their own breathing.

When I am teaching, I direct the class to be mindful of their breath in an intentional sort of way. This is a regular teaching in my yoga and meditation classes, to use the 2 × 6 sticky mat or meditation cushion as your training ground for mindful mental discipline, but it could just as easily be anywhere you are. No mat or special equipment is necessary. Breathing may sound mundane, but it will go on with or without your attention. If you give it no attention, it will likely be shallow or erratic, and you will start to dream or worry about things which are not happening at that moment, like what you'll do after class, or what you'll make for dinner. These are things that have a time and place for attention, but not when you are trying to give some love and attention to your health and peace of mind. I remind my students not to give away their precious practice time by permitting their mind to wander around.

Projecting images onto a mind that hasn't gotten any direction yet is like driving a car with no GPS: if you don't pay attention to where you're going, you'll end up far from your destination. I assure you that if peace of mind is your intended destination, give attention to breathing with depth and ease, then your body and brain will feel very good. Small things will start to feel joyful. I encourage breathing with great interest, so that it is impossible to miss this important part of your life. The day you can no longer have a breath to enjoy is the day you no longer have a breath, so don't miss it!

Zen Buddhist Master Thich Nhat Hanh is well known for his teachings of present moment enjoyment in simple tasks such as drinking tea. The enjoyment is in the process, not merely in the act of putting fluid down your throat. The enjoyment starts in the very first step of choosing the tea. Observe each step mindfully: preparing the boiling water, pouring the water, and waiting a minute for the tea to cool are all moments to enjoy. When you are practicing a mindful activity such as tea making, you can affirm in your mind what exactly it is that you are doing so you don't get ahead of yourself: "I am making tea. I am stirring the tea. I am sitting and drinking the tea." Sounds simple. But when you know you are drinking tea— and I mean really know this through your direct experience— you will also know what you are not doing, and that is an important distinction during healing. Intentional healing experiences are a key component to peace of mind and maintaining health. When a spiritual download occurs, return to the safety and calm of what is actually happening right now, which in the simplest terms is just sitting down, reading, drinking your tea, and breathing in and out. Whatever you are doing in the moment, try to stay present as you are doing it.

Mindful Breathing

Sit comfortably and close your eyes. Enjoy a sigh—it releases tension. Take three slow, deliberate breaths. Enjoy the feeling of cool air inside the nose on the way in, and the warmth of the air on the way out. Continue breathing only through the nose, unless blocked sinuses prevent you from breathing comfortably. Take a slow and full inhale, and pause momentarily at the top of the in-breath. Then exhale fully, but not forcefully. Do this a couple of times with no gasping or harshness in the throat. Settle into a comfortable breathing rhythm that suits you. Bring your attention to the expansion in your rib cage when you breathe in, and the softening or settling down of the rib cage and shoulders when you breathe out. After you've been breathing mindfully for a couple of minutes, notice if there is any residual tension in your body. Refine your sitting position and continue to breathe in a manner that helps you feel comfortable and relaxed. Release tension in your body as it arises to your attention. Just be. Allow yourself to just sit without having to do anything else. Give yourself permission to be right where you are, doing exactly what you're doing. Open your eyes and smile from the heart when you are ready to resume your activity, or to shift your focus and attention on another sense such as touch, taste, or smell.

Mindful Hearing

Have a Mindful Moment by listening to birdsong nearby. You can hear their chirps and calls, but your mind has no desire to announce the details nor label the experience with words. You can hear without thinking about what you are hearing, or reacting to the birdsong. You are just hearing. A non-mindful experience would be thinking about what kind of bird it is, whether it's migration season, or about the bird feeder that you had prepared in your backyard the previous weekend. These are all unneeded descriptions that detract from the experience of hearing the birdsong. The fewer details in your mind's description of the experience, the closer it is likely to be a present moment experience. Keep it simple.

Mindful Eating

Turn off nearby electronics and gadgets or put them out of reach. Music with no lyrics, such as jazz or classical, can be an enjoyable experience while eating a mindful meal. Thank the provider or preparer of the meal sincerely either verbally or from your heart. Take a look at the arrangement of food on the plate. Notice the colors and textures on your plate. This creates an appreciation for the attention and artistry of food preparation. It does not have to be a fancy meal to appreciate how foods come together to create tastes and textures. Before you take the first bite, breathe deeply to take in the aroma of the plate of food before you. If you had a stressful day, do a little mindful breathing before you begin eating. Over all, it's better to be relaxed before you eat than have indigestion later. Chew each bite with great interest in the tastes and textures. Mindful eating can also include, if appropriate, inquiring between bites how it was prepared, special ingredients, or the history of the recipe. It doesn't have to be a game of Twenty Questions, but having the table conversation with the attention on the food rather than controversial news or other un-settling topics may contribute to feelings of gratitude and harmony towards the person who prepared it.

Notice how you feel after that last bite is eaten, and also two hours later when you have partially digested what you ate. Enjoy the satisfaction of fulfilling a basic human need with nourishing, life-giving food. Take the time to appreciate the cycle of arising hunger, food preparation, smell, touch, taste, and, finally, satisfac-tion with the meal. In many spiritual and cultural traditions, paying respect to your food—including its source, its care, its preparation, and its consummation—is a highly spiritual practice and is also grounding, meaning that nourishing food feels balancing. Mindful Mealtimes are an important moment of gratitude for many people, for we cannot survive nor thrive without nourishment. If you are just starting a mindfulness practice, I encourage using mealtimes as a time to notice when hunger arises, the food choices you make to attain nourishment, and how you feel during and after you eat.

Mindful Seeing

Observing nature brings peace to the mind so we should take the opportunity to use our eyes to enjoy the color and movement of our natural surroundings. Whether it's a grove of trees nearby, a garden, or a simple potted plant, living things inspire us to live with peace and vitality. Look around to find something that is growing nearby. When you find your object of focus, relax your eyes and observe its shape and structure. Trace its form and follow any movement it makes without analyzing it. Observe the colors and shades made by light and shadow. Feel free to blink and even close your eyes for a bit, but stay with it. If you prefer something with movement, I recommend fish tanks (watch just one fish), clouds, and tall trees in the breeze. Take a few deep breaths and stay present with your visual object. Set a timer if you need to get back to an activity, or let the session end when you feel calm and centered.

As you can tell from the poem about the pinecone turning into a Saint Bernard, the mind doesn't always stay put the first time you try. Imagination, worries, or delusions can take over when we are not in control of the mind, but practice will make it easier and more enjoyable. I wrote the poem at the beginning of this chapter a few weeks into working on my mindfulness practice alone in my room at a retreat center. I was in a good mood and allowed my mind to be more playful, but I still found it quite amusing that my imagination took over and created a Saint Bernard out of a pinecone! I wrote my observations in my journal which turned into that poem. My practice at that time was to be fully present with each sense, and that day it was my sense of sight. I was inspired to explore my senses more fully by a book written by Jon Kabat-Zinn titled *Coming to Your Senses* starting with taste, then touch, then sight, and finally closing my eyes to enjoy my sense of hearing. The book took me on a journey of exploring my senses, but with some restraint and discipline over which sense I was using. The poem is a reminder that I have to cultivate a beginner's mind no matter how many years I have been practicing. There is no graduation from the school of mindfulness! The mind is in constant need of a framework in which to enjoy our humanity. The five senses are a wonderful place to start learning about placing our attention on one object, so I recommend doing at least one of these mindfulness exercises daily. Living your life more mindfully will discipline you to be mindful in most of your activities, discernment of past, present, and future will come more easily, and processing spiritual information will be less burdensome.

Becoming aware and enjoying your immediate surroundings is an important step towards discernment of what is in your mind versus what is happening on the ground. This is an important distinction if you are burdened by anxiety, because anxiousness about the future is a non-mindful activity. When we are mindful of the present moment, there is no room to be nervous about what has not happened. The single-pointed focus of grounding yourself in the present is a stepping stone toward focusing on other issues that you wish to explore one at a time.

Mindfulness to meditation can seem like a big jump from thinking about a flower to imagining yourself as a flower, or hearing a bird and then feeling yourself flying above the treetops with the birds in your mind, but it's really just an extension of the same thing. Meditation is an act of focusing your mind in one direction, on one thing, with no distractions, for a sustained period of time. That may sound like a tall order, but to gain wisdom and insight from spiritual information, meditation is a necessity. We all have to start somewhere, and that place is to be mindful.

10

MEDITATION

STRUGGLING MORNING MEDITATION

5am. The house is dark.
I light a candle and find my seat.
My ankles itch.
I'm cold.
I get a blanket and wrap up inside it.
I pull it like a cloak around me and over my head.
But I cannot disappear from myself.
I watch my thoughts wander around.
I point one out to myself
"See! A thought! What is it doing?"
I make it sit down and be quiet.
Then comes another.

My eyes get hot from tears in the dark
For my earth mother who will not console me
My fear, my anger, my restless mind,
My constant activity was all to not feel her distance, disapproval,
disgust
With me
Breath starts, stops, sobs again and again
But I have an answer. I know I can do this.
At least I know what I have been hiding from all along.

I see light.
The light has no words and no judgment.
It is quiet.
The light glows and shimmers as a veil is lifted.
The light of an eternity showed itself to me
For only half a minute.
But it is there now, which is the only thing that matters:
Forty-five minutes out of a lifetime in the dark
to see the light.

For the first few months following the years-long crisis with my health, I rededicated myself to slowing down and taking better care of myself; however, I was still quite easily distracted. I felt like my mind was a mess of tangled knots and frayed loose threads. When I learned to focus through mindfulness and in greater depth through meditation, I was finally able to direct my attention towards what I felt was important: education, self-study, and goals for my future. Extending my focused mindfulness into longer meditation sessions helped me to practice focusing on one thing, something that had eluded me in school. Whenever education or new skills were required to level up, I froze up. I was tired of feeling anxious and eager to explore my mind's potential. I could no longer lean on any argument that I was learning-impaired or that teachers didn't care enough to teach me; it was going to be my responsibility for learning and finding the right teachers, and to practice what I learned. It was the greatest feeling to know that if I could dedicate myself to focus on something long enough to master it, I could learn virtually anything I wanted!

I found many benefits to being more mindful such as mental clarity, enjoyment of normal everyday things, and a reduction in reactivity to toxic people in my life. Once I tamed my monkey mind I began to have better control over my thoughts, emotions, and reactions. As I "detoxed" my friend list, I had more time to focus on high quality relationships and my education. My focus improved on nearly any topic of interest, which boosted my self-esteem and confidence to continue learning. My endurance to sit in quiet for extended periods of time also grew, which one day sparked my interest to an enduring question that had always been lurking in the back of my consciousness: "What is my purpose here?" I was stumped over this inner inquiry, lingering for a time near the Gate of Oneness with my heart and mind beloved to All That Is, but I had to keep in mind that I was also a mother and a part of a family who loved me. I couldn't be a good role model for my children and also wander off to a cave somewhere or become a monk so I needed to link my purpose to something that would also benefit my family and my future. I re-connected to a defined purpose here on earth by shifting my focus toward compassion and the relief of suffering of others.

Mindfulness and meditation share some important qualities, but they are not the same. There are many ways to enter into meditation such as repeating a sacred word called a mantra, or repeating an action, such as a breath pattern or a rhythmic movement such as drumming, dance, or even rocking in a rocking chair! Mindfulness is a simple, non-religious way to enter into meditation when there is something deeper that you'd like to have greater wisdom about, which is a part of the integration process when healing from spiritual crisis and awakening. Think of mindfulness as a gateway or path, and meditation is the gate itself.

Objects of meditation are endless; they are as numerous as objects themselves or any image or person you can conjure up in your mind. Your object of meditation may dawn on you through mindfulness, or you may consciously choose it, but whatever you choose should be chosen carefully. As an example, you can be mindful of a single bird chirping outside, but meditating on a chirping bird may not help you to achieve your goal of being a peaceful person. Being mindful as you eat will help mealtimes be more enjoyable, and may help us to also appreciate the causes and conditions that grow and prepare our food, but meditating on food is unlikely to help you understand your spiritual gifts. But if you meditate on your heart center, you may discover a powerful energy within you that is useful for creating better relationships. Mindfulness of our own energies, then meditation on discernment between our thoughts and emotions and that of others is helpful for creating safe and effective relationship boundaries and reducing miscommunication and misunderstanding. Mindfulness of our mental and emotional state can bring about a meditation on how to more effectively use our energy, or even to do less so that we can be happy more!

Meditation is a deep impression of a quality or set of qualities that you wish to make a part of you and that is an important task. It can be done on your own, but receiving guidance from an experienced teacher is worth every minute and hour that you spend learning how to do it. The depth and meaning of your meditations are notable when you choose an appropriate object or topic of meditation with someone who knows you and your personal and spiritual goals well. Whether meditating upon the qualities of a holy human being, a deity, god, goddess, or Mother Nature, your meditation should feel natural, and enhance your feelings of wellbeing. If you do a meditation that leaves you feeling sleepy or mentally dull, excessively superior or magnanimous, spaced out, or in opposition to others, you should consider changing your object of meditation. Meditation, when done well, will prepare your mind for learning just about anything, can improve any skill set, and help you to integrate the flow of information from spiritual sources. When meditation is mastered you will not only have the five or six senses that most people inherently have, but you will likely have additional spiritual knowledge that might appear magical, mystical, or healing to others who are not in touch with this energy.

If you've made a decision to stay awake *and* do your best to be in harmony with others—despite the stress you will feel just by being around other people—meditation is the next step. One of the toughest challenges of awakening is staying grounded and connected to others, especially because as your views change you won't see eye to eye with many people. Learning to meditate will help you be less reactive to what others say and do and to care a little less about what others think about you, which should relieve some stress. Mindfulness and meditation really are essential forms of self-care.

When I decided to start taking this meditation thing seriously, I had to find out what I was thinking and feeling that was driving me to chaos and poor health. My teacher had been telling me this for a long time, and now it was time to dig deep. I knew from my Buddhist studies that a cluttered mind was an obstacle to spiritual progress, so I had my intention. I also pulled from my experience with Western-style business success-coaching that setting up the proper space and equipment is necessary to ensure follow-through with my intention. But I was not in a group class, and my teacher was not in my living room. I was really going to do this all alone in the actual sitting still, and that was terrifying to me.

As I have mentioned before, I find the most value in finding my own teachers, some of whom I have met or heard teach in person or read their books. A few of my teachers are world famous, such as the 14th Dalai Lama, but most are householders with a job and a family just like myself. I tend to favor meeting with teachers or listening to them speak over heavy coursework and formal trainings. When I found a qualified mentor who embodied the qualities I wanted to grow within myself, I wanted to learn about their personal practice so I could develop one for myself. I never specifically asked any one of my teachers to teach me how to meditate during any of our meetings, but every one of them did in their own way. Meditation techniques are a formality I am happy to do away with once I no longer need them, and I tell this to anyone who is just learning to meditate. Anyone can read about yoga and meditation, but a role model is priceless. They show the way by how they live, and by sharing how they get results. If they are alive today, they probably still do some form of yoga or meditation because it is a part of their life, just as they encouraged me to make it a part of my own. The best teachers live their daily life in a state of yoga, meaning that what they say, do, think, and feel cannot be separate or parsed from how they live. When you find someone who has the qualities you wish to embody—healthy, happy, compassionate, etcetera—that person may be a good teacher or role model for you. I cannot overemphasize the benefits of having a role model and inspiration for doing a personal practice to my personal growth and spiritual development. I credit the guidance of a good teacher, an acharya, who has lived through crisis and awakening and could relate to my struggles. It is to this end that I am writing this now—that my experience has congealed and solidified into something I could teach to others and contribute to the greater good.

I do not follow one pure method, but I do have great teachers. I give great credit to significant authors, podcasters, community teachers, seminar leaders, and excellent online sources for a great deal of my continued education. I did not divine my education, but I am mostly self-taught where it comes to how I practice yoga and meditation. When I decided to regularly do a sitting practice to find out what was in my head, I had plenty of information about "how" to start, but I lacked discipline or a routine to go beyond a single sitting. It was discouraging to be so impatient and fidgety, but I was determined to dig deeper into my human nature, my emotional boundaries, and to heal my inner wounds.

The night before I was to start, I picked out a special space to sit in my living room, and carefully chose the items I needed for meditation success! I placed a blank writing journal and a sharpened pencil next to my new purple buckwheat-hull zafu cushion on my space on the living room floor. The Dalai Lama meditates long before sunrise, so I felt I had my heart in the right place by setting my alarm clock for 5am before I settled into bed. I shared with my husband my plans to meditate before sunrise. The stifled chuckle I heard in the dark indicated his disbelief that I could follow through with such a plan, knowing full well that I love to sleep and cannot even speak until well after 7am. The in-the-dark conversation went like this:

Husband: "So, tomorrow's the day you start meditating?"

Me: "Well, I'll wake up at five, but chime-time is 5:15am. I have to wake up a bit before I sit."

Husband: "Chime time?"

Me: "I found this website called Tree Leaf Zendo where lay-Buddhists can meditate and receive guidance from a Roshi (teacher) anywhere in the world. When you click 'Meditate,' a little chime signals the start and end of the sitting. Oh, and they burn a virtual incense stick that is exactly as long as the sitting. I can watch the thing burn while I sit to pass the time."

Husband: "Good luck." He's so positive for my sake.

Me: "I have to sit before the baby wakes up or I really have no chance. The day gets going, and I'll forget, so it's the only time I have to do it. And I have to do it."

Husband: "I see. Good luck, honey. Good night."

I woke up the next morning at 5am on a new journey to self-discovery! I put a cool washcloth on my face, drank a glass of lemon water that I kept on my bedside table, and hustled out to turn on my computer and log into my supportive online virtual tribe. I thought a 15-minute stick of incense should be enough time to set my mind straight. I settled onto the cushion, set my posture, and then dimmed my eyes to the virtual incense stick on my computer monitor.

The very first minute I experienced a parade of thoughts. I felt an itch on my foot. Should I resist scratching it, or give it a scratch? Then I felt tickle on my forehead. I reached up and rubbed it. Then I felt hungry. I looked at the time. (it HAD to be at least 10 minutes, didn't it?) It had been barely four minutes. Well, I scratched and fidgeted, ached and agitated—and the chime finally tinkled its sound of sweet relief that I had survived my crazy mind for a full ten minutes.

I proceeded to write it all down in short, choppy, agitated pen-smeared printing so I would know, once and for all, what was making me unable to sit still. I took a look at what I wrote. It was all a bunch of distractions from realizing my actual state of mind. Never mind that I had a profoundly spiritual awakening when I was six but at this early hour I clearly could not handle ten minutes of quiet with myself.

Although brief at first, I had a revelation about myself every single time I sat to meditate. The 5am sittings did not last long, but I had disciplined myself for two solid weeks to get up and figure out how to sit and be still. This was the foundation of a less formal, but more frequent, meditation practice I learned to fit into my life which I have observed ever since. I simply cannot do without it. The duration of my meditations was determined by how long the baby would nap after I finished a load of laundry, or a little sitting time in between teaching a yoga class and returning phone calls and emails. This was the kind of loose structure that worked for me so that meditation would never again be put off due to work or family.

My advice to anyone going through awakening or crisis is that you should try to sit and be still on a regular basis, even for a few minutes every day. If you absolutely cannot sit still, choose a moving meditation such as yoga, chi gong, or even a spontaneous dance—whatever movement feels right and comfortable for you, then try to sit still. That stillness and quiet will eventually become a safe haven for you.

A Buddhist orders a veggie-dog, "One with everything," he says. He pays the vendor with a $20 bill. The vendor takes the money, hands him the food, and continues his work. The Buddhist is confused as he waits for his change. The vendor replies, "Change must come from within."

~Zen Buddhist joke

11

YOGA

*Yoga is a way of moving into stillness in order to
experience the truth of who you are.*

~Erich Schiffman, from
Yoga: The Spirit and Practice of Moving into Stillness

When a person is experiencing pain or suffering, yoga is not usually the first place people look to feel better. It is fairly common that a person will try yoga and meditation only after they've tried many other medical or alternative options. When looking for help, people usually seek out doctors and therapists, but yoga is coming to be known as an effective alternative and complementary healing activity with great potential for interpersonal change. Erratic or imbalanced energy can cause a variety of physical maladies such as headaches and constipation, or emotional disturbances such as anxiety, sadness, confusion, and insomnia. With the huge amount of stress that our families, workplace, and success-driven society place on us, it's no wonder—we need yoga more than ever!

Many people are going in droves to talk it out in therapy and go to doctors for prescription medications to make the bad feelings go away. But it's getting more complicated than that. The medical solution does not always befit the malady. If an imbalance has gone on for too long without relief, both physical pain and emotional suffering will occur no matter which came first. This is how I have come to meet hundreds of people whose feelings of discontentment and anxiety were adversely affecting their health.

Although I have heard from some people who have experienced sudden spontaneous awakenings, and read other accounts of spiritual emergency requiring acute, immediate attention in a clinical setting, the stories I present to you are not as extreme. I do not treat any medical conditions. If an individual is unable to care for themselves, or require acute psychiatric or medical care, that would be out of my scope of practice. The stories I present are from people who walked into my office on their own free will, and were able to care for themselves and handle daily tasks. Some had been prescribed pharmaceuticals and called to meet with me with the ink still wet on the script in their pocket.

Yoga is both a process and a state of being. Yoga is a physical activity as well as the result of that activity. There are a multitude of sources to learn different methods of yoga, and yoga centers where teachers provide group classes and education on this healing art. There are also DVDs, YouTube videos, and online streaming classes at your fingertips, but not one of these can tell you what kind of yoga is appropriate or even safe for you. Consulting an experienced teacher face-to-face is one of the more reliable ways to receive instruction, but face-to-face nowadays can be a Skype session or video chat. A competent teacher should get a brief health history, have an idea of your goals for practice, assess your breathing, and guide you into movements that are appropriate for you based on what they know about you and your needs. If a teacher cannot or will not assess you, you must know that you are the master of your own body, and it is only through experimenting with the practice that you will arrive at the practice that is right for you.

When new students come to see me for private lessons in yoga, I listen to them and answer any questions they have about what a breath-centered practice is like. There is a little paperwork where

I ask for brief health history and a few questions that will lead to more information about their diet, sleep habits, activity level, and stress management. I consult with them about their needs and goals using my heightened and developed senses to learn about them personally and energetically. Most of the time, a new student who has guarded and covered their illness or suffering for years can sense that I have no defenses towards them and will let their guard down, too. Letting go of emotional defenses is a continued practice for me so that I do not transfer any suffering to others. I also practice an energetic fortification that surrounds me in a blue egg so that I do not accumulate anyone else's suffering. The emotional defense release sometimes comes with a few tears for first-time clients, but not every time, and clients often state that they feel much better even after just a few minutes with me. This comes from my daily compassion meditation and reiki energy work practice that I do before I even meet them, not from any ritual or special counsel when they are there with me.

When a student is really ready to be seen for who they are and to receive guidance toward what they want for their lives, they are much more likely to practice what I teach them. The typical tools are of yoga and mindfulness: time-tested and well researched techniques that calm the nervous system and are beneficial for overall health and wellbeing. I then design a practice for their specific needs which can bring relief in just a few weeks or months of practice, depending on how often they practice plus additional self-care and improvement of lifestyle habits. The outcomes are nearly always more significant when the student practices at home or in guided classes with experienced teachers who are aware of the process of spiritual awakening.

However, occasionally a client or yoga student who has enjoyed relatively good health is uncertain from where their emotional (and later, physical) discomfort arose. Following several years of dedicated practice, it became clearer to me that the conflicts I was hearing from my students and clients were not simply health related for which they were seeking a physical solution. Nor were they merely expressing emotional problems for which they were seeking guidance in stress reduction and meditation. Clients were more commonly appearing as a serious mess of dysfunctional empathy, anxiety, and overloaded with extra-sensory input. These are not conditions of only the mind, or only of the body, but a combination of the two.

Add to that spiritual information that is extremely difficult to communicate to others, this can create a situation that needs special understanding and care. And it wasn't until I came to understand my own process of crisis and awakening that I was able to see it in others. It took me a long time to successfully navigate these issues myself, but I never found *anyone* who could explain this trifecta of complications of empathy, anxiety, and extra-sensory input, or advise me how to resolve them for good.

My first awareness of what a spiritual crisis might look like in another person came about 10 years after I had started teaching. A few of my yoga students were experiencing a lot of anxiety and emotional instability. (With respect to the privacy of my clients and students, real names and confidential information has been omitted or changed.) Stacy was a suburban middle-aged mother of teenagers, feeling anxious and uneasy about the traditional paradigms of the media, medicine, and mothering. She felt herself starting to pull away from her usual groups of friends and associations hoping to find a tribe of people dealing with similar issues. She represents a growing population of women who want to make a positive change in the world and in their life, but feel terribly uncertain about how to proceed. She had considered herself a bright, confident person, but her view had started to shift as she was experiencing some health problems and filled with doubt and dread about the future. It wasn't until Stacy and I connected through reflections on her yoga and meditation practice that I suspected the challenges she was facing stemmed from having a gradual and progressive spiritual awakening. As we worked together, I tried to help her understand that although she was having a hard time adjusting, this was going to be a very good thing for her family and connections in her community.

Another time, one of my regular class students asked for a private session with me to sort out some uneasy feelings. I was developing a yoga sequence protocol for anxiety which I taught to him and seemed to help some, but not entirely. Over a period of time, David had greater awareness of the suffering the had been building up over several months which was now preventing him from enjoying life. He was in a constant state of anxiety, worry, digestive pain, and was having trouble sleeping. Using the tools of yoga and mindfulness, he developed a greater awareness of the source of his depression and anxiety, and what he told me very closely resembled an empath in spiritual crisis. An empath is someone who feels the emotions of other people quite strongly, to the degree that they have difficulty distinguishing their own emotions from those of others.

Following the consultation, we developed an appropriate yoga and mindfulness practice which over time would help him to overcome his primary challenge: to discern his own feelings from those of others. Slowing down and learning to be more mindful helped him to reduce stress as well. The practice I recommended daily over a period of several months was successful to the point that he was able to be more mindful, reduce stress, and self-regulate his moods. But other pivotal realizations occurred as he sorted out the cause of anxiety that could bring the strongest person to their knees: his relationship to the entire world was changing, and his new perspective was causing conflict in his marriage. He was realizing a stronger connection to nature and the environment, questioning the role of God in this world, and disliking his job.

David's entire worldview was shaken to the core with no comprehension about where his feelings were coming from. When he came to me for help, he was not seeking to make major life changes, he only wished to feel calm and peaceful, and to sleep well at night.

Although this triad of health issues, anxiety, and a perpetual fear of death are similar to what we might call a midlife crisis, they are also a symptom of spiritual crisis that cannot be quelled by a fancy new car or other such upgrade in lifestyle appearance. Prior to this he had no experience, tools, or support structure to help him process all of these new feelings that were coming into him. It was like being buried in an avalanche under 20 feet of suffocating snow.

Fear is the broth that stews the bitter poisonous soup of anxiety. And nothing is more terrifying than the fear of the unknown. People fear what will happen if they follow their heart and change careers and losing relationships built over years. They fear losing faith and losing their identity. They fear being consumed by anger, grief, and loss. All of this fear and anxiety is caused when our views change over a relatively short period of time based on a new perspective, new information, and new feelings. It might not be so bad to happen slowly, but Spirit doesn't work by our calendar. When a huge spiritual download of information comes flying in, we can feel overburdened and overwhelmed. I explained this trifecta of symptoms of a spiritual crisis and asked if that sounded like a reasonable explanation for how he was feeling. It was a relief when David laughed out loud and said, "You mean I'm *not* crazy?!"

I discovered this pattern again and again with students experiencing this trifecta of troubles. In working with each of these students and clients toward recognizing what their journey is all about, they express a sense of relief that they are not going crazy, no matter how intense or illogical they may feel. I assure them that they will be able to function here on earth and navigate healthy relationships with people and with the Divine once and for all. There is hope.

The ancient Indian sage Patanjali was the first person to write down the path of yoga about 400CE. His writings are one of the primary sources of yogic wisdom and philosophy that are still widely studied and practiced today. The teachings of Patanjali, or yoga sutra, eloquently explains in a mere 196 lines in four chapters *why* we should seek yoga as a path to unite with universal spirit, but it is indeed a heady, complex text few people want to study when healing from a spiritual awakening, so I will get to the gist of my best takeaways from the teachings so you don't have to.

Yoga is not just something you do; it is a state of mind-body integration where you feel good, your mind is clear and light, and you are in a state of open-minded concentration on one thing. I have used the example of breathing as a convenient and always available object of meditation, but once you are in a state of yoga—the full yoga—you may focus on anything you wish. Yoga has physical, mental, and spiritual applications, but it is not a religion. Yoga is meant to be adapted to the individual, taking into consideration a person's physical abilities, stage of life, their temperament, and their goals for practice. It is for this reason that I am not in favor of the large-scale group fitness classes labeled as yoga so prevalent today, and that curious new students should take some time to find an experienced teacher and inquire about how they teach yoga.

Yoga is an ancient Sanskrit word meaning "to unite" or "to join" which refers to our connection to Spirit as well as our connection to our bodies, and to the hearts and souls of our fellow beings on this planet. Many sufferings can be abated if we can avoid more separation and work to create more connections among people, especially where it comes to individuals and groups who disagree or do not see the world in the same way. Realize that the more you awaken, the more you will realize who is not awake, and this will cause you some disappointment. But just as you found your own way to the Light, we must hold that Light for others to see, even if they never do. In some ways, spiritual awakening can be the event that causes division—but in the end it is your choice to turn away from those in the dark, or you can decide to hold compassion alive as everyone finds their way to the Light in their own way. Yoga is one powerfully effective way to arrive at this compassionate view.

Yoga relates to the balance of opposing forces in our bodies, our minds, and our hearts. Yoga can help to relieve much of the suffering that we humans have to deal with: anger and disappointment from attachment, self-doubt from ignorance, and over-consumption from craving. Living a life without yoga is fraught with the pushing and pulling of opposing forces and a feeling of being constantly out of balance and out of control. This can lead to a prolonged struggle to not only control and manipulate others, but also to a feeling of guilt and shame for not being able to behave better and be a "good" person more often, even when you know you are not a "bad" person. When you have joined the opposites of your being, you will feel whole and healed.

Every person has to approach dealing with these opposing forces in their own way, but I specifically recommend yoga because it offers several ways to heal the physical body, emotional and mental anguish, and spiritual doubt: the trifecta of a spiritual crisis. Additionally, yoga has a component that I feel is unique to the healing and integration process of relationship connection: yoga awakens compassion.

While you are undergoing a period of healing, there can be some misunderstanding and tension even in the closest of families. You may not understand everything that you are going through during your awakening and family members can misunderstand or mistrust your needs. Yoga can help you moderate your needs and speak clearly and truthfully to others so your needs and the needs of your nearest and dearest can be understood. If a person feels that their point of view is the only valid way to see something, there is no compassion there and relationship is cut off. If we push our views and perceptions on someone who is not ready to understand, we need to accept that person cannot or does not wish to understand at that time. If someone is unkind or insensitive when you share about yourself, do not take it personally. You must accept that your journey has afforded you an understanding and a wisdom that they do not have at this time. You will probably recall a time when you were ignorant, angry, or fearful of something that caused you to have an incorrect view or to behave inappropriately. Allow compassion to arise for yourself and the other person from this recollection. If we practice the heart of yoga in its true sense—union and connection—we should integrate the truth of another person into our view so compassion is possible. Otherwise we are just judging everyone's ignorance and insensitivity all the time which doesn't feel good at all and does nothing to create harmony and connection among people. We not only need to unite our mind-body-spirit for the greatest amount of healing in our journey, but join and unite in a shared love and compassion for the journey of others—even if, and especially when, we do not agree. I prefer to think of yoga as a removal of obstacles so that every part of my existence feels balanced. From this perspective, yoga is not a way of fixing something wrong with me or the other person, but a kind of harmonization and integration of a peaceful way of being that does not separate me from others regardless of our views.

As awakening beings, it is in our best interests to not separate entirely from others. I believe that it is in the best interests of humanity to remove obstacles to understanding, and create opportunity for connection when the time is right. Regardless of one's culture or religious background, we know in our hearts that discovering, or re-discovering this union or harmony with God or Universal Source is a primary goal, and when All Are One that includes everyone.

The tradition of yoga that has been adapted for the west is quite secular: it does not describe a god we must win favor from, nor does it promise a heavenly reward. The true power of yoga lies in the power of mastery over the body and all mental activity. The essential wisdom is distilled into the teachings of most experienced yoga teachers and explain the specific methods and beneficial outcomes of unifying the mind, body, and spirit. Practicing yoga really can be as simple as moving your body and breathing in a safe, deliberate, and mindful manner. It also has the capacity to transform your consciousness so that each individual can reach their highest aspiration of unifying with God.

'Pranayama' is the word used in yoga to mean gaining control of your life-force through breathing. Physiologically, breathing is closely related to nervous system activity in both the "fight or flight" stress response and "rest and digest" recovery response. When you are breathing rapidly or erratically, mental activity also tends to be erratic and unfocused. When breathing becomes smooth and slow during mindfulness practice, you are able to more easily slow down mental activity. When you breathe in, pay attention to the small pause at the top of your breath before the exhale starts. You'll notice there is also a pause at the end of your exhale before the next inhale begins. During these brief periods of no-thought and no-action, your mind can begin to anticipate these pauses and enjoy the space that is created there. If you practice breathing while observing these pauses and no thoughts arise in the pause, you can extend that mental quietude into the rest of the breathing cycle. Less thought and more quiet equals more healing time. These pauses are the doorway to concentrate on just one thing that is personal to you in meaning and intention, which for me was compassion.

The path of yoga starts with gaining control over the body which we could interpret as "mastering" our physical health and sustaining our attention on the well-being of our bodies. That is not to say that you cannot meditate until you are perfectly healthy. But if you have health issues that would make it complicated or impossible to sustain your attention on something other than pain or discomfort in your body, the perfect place to start is to cultivate a smooth, steady breath and meditate on that. We cannot master what we cannot pay attention to, so when you sit to be still and breathe, as mundane or boring as you may think, it will become a sacred doorway for you to gain greater control of your energy, thoughts, feelings, and actions.

Inhale, and God approaches you. Hold the inhalation, and God remains with you. Exhale, and you approach God. Hold the exhalation, and surrender to God.
~T. Krishnamacharya

12

CARING THROUGH CRISIS: ADRIANNE'S JOURNEY

Six years ago, I had a grand mal seizure which set into motion three years of health struggles and turned my world upside down. In the months that followed, I experienced anxiety attacks on a regular basis, numbness in my extremities, dizziness, extreme fatigue and depression, as well as heightened sensitivity to just about everything. While my physical body was unpredictable, I was mentally and emotionally unstable, and felt completely out of control. I was terrified that I would never gain back my stability and frustrated with the lack of answers from traditional Western Medicine about my condition. There was such a mystery to these events; I knew there were deeper lessons to be learned, and soul searching to be done, thus began my path to healing. I began reading articles and watching videos about chakras and energy medicine, the Emotional Freedom Technique (tapping on acupressure points) and Reiki. I took classes in Qigong, Pranic Healing, Tai Chi, spiritual healing, meditation, and sound and crystal healing, among others. I joined a yoga studio and took every class possible. I went to see an energy doctor and acupuncturist, a Chiropractor, Naturopath and Homeopathic doctor. Over the course of the next three years, and with a lot of love and support from friends and family, I slowly regained my sense of self and stability.

Five years after my seizure, I was in Reiki Level 2 training when life threw another curve ball at me, only this time it didn't happen to me personally, but to loved ones of mine. Within a few weeks of each other, I received news that a dear friends' cancer was terminal, and my sweet little 5-year-old niece was diagnosed with Acute Lymphoblastic Leukemia. I was devastated, as were my family and friends. The fear, grief and pain were constant and palpable. Having been in such a fragile state myself just a few years prior, I questioned my ability to handle these situations. Coming to grips with this new reality was extremely difficult, but I knew I needed to be strong for my loved ones. I also knew it was ok to let the tears flow and feel the intensity of my emotions, instead of trying to cut them off like I had been doing my whole life. It became clear to me that my recent health journey was going to be what carried me through these experiences. The spiritual, emotional, physical and holistic work I did prior to these traumatic situations provided me a foundation of faith, strength and self-love, which helped me stay grounded.

To help myself through this difficult time, I took yoga and meditation classes whenever possible, and did mindfulness exercises on my own. In addition, I used homeopathic remedies and essential oils to support my nervous system, practiced the Emotional Freedom Technique, and listened to Abraham Hicks' Law of Attraction lessons. During the toughest times when I was feeling extremely sad and scared, I prayed often, and practiced Reiki on my my niece, our family, my ill friend and myself. At one point during a yin yoga class while in a sustained restoration pose, I experienced some telling images that helped me come to terms with the current crises. After that class, I felt a sense of peace that I hadn't previously had. I don't think this would have been possible without the inner work I'd done.

In addition, I've made a career change into a healing profession by training in a type of bodywork called Restorative Muscle Therapy, so that I can help others on their own path to health and wholeness. Lastly, I made a concerted effort to speak to friends and others about my loved ones battling cancer, which I never would have had the strength to do in the past. I truly believe in the power of love, prayers and positive thoughts.

This journey has evolved the way I look at and experience life. All of the restorative work has led me to a place of acceptance, and I am now better equipped to not only help myself, but those around me in need. The immersion into therapeutic modalities such as yoga, meditation, and energy work after my seizure alleviated the stress in my nervous system, and my brain and body slowly began to heal. I truly believe this is the reason I am doing as well as I am today. I am a highly sensitive person, which has led to difficulties with boundaries, and feelings of vulnerability and weakness for much of my life, and now I have a much stronger foundation. Though I still struggle, this allows me solid ground on which to stand, even when presented with challenging situations, as was the case this past year. I have faith that no matter what life brings, I will be able to manage my way through it, and help others along the way.

13

THE QUEST FOR
HIGHER PURPOSE

SAMSARA

I suffer.
I worry about crowded homes, no homes
Hungry bodies, starving spirits
I feel too cold, too hot
No comfort.
Every day is the same or worse.
In my tight little mind,
Suffering is my poverty of choice
I have everything to share
but I worry constantly about what I have
and grieve daily my losses
and double my suffering with the cries of others
as I sit quietly with my own.

When you come to understand the causes and conditions that create suffering, you will no longer be bound by it. While you are not likely to forget the weight of pain and suffering you have endured, your healing practice will transform your perception of the events and you will not suffer with it anymore. When you take responsibility for your breathing, mindfulness, and state of health, the possibility of having a higher purpose begins to open up and the suffering mindset dwindles away. With the right support and healing time, you will come to understand the purpose for this journey to discover more freedom and clarity that may not have been present before. Out of that inner freedom may emerge a feeling that your journey—the crisis, the suffering, the process of healing—was for a greater purpose, and now the call to do something bigger can be heard and answered. You can start to be the master of your own destiny and create a life you enjoy living!

Ask yourself now, "what will I do when I am no longer in pain?"

Living life with purpose means finding out what are your unique strengths, talents, or special senses and use them to educate, serve, or heal others in some way for a purpose beyond your own needs. What you do with your natural-born talents and hard-earned skills are a personal choice to either share, save, or squander, but the world does need you and it will appreciate your contribution for a greater purpose than daily living tasks. A limited purpose would be performing daily functions such as sleeping, eating, taking care of family members, getting a compulsory education, and going to work as a means to make money to survive. Daily activities of caretaking, education, work, and even leisure hobbies are not merely modern-living survival tasks; they can become fulfilling aspirations to achieve a greater purpose.

Deciding to serve the world also serves you and those closest to you because we are All One. Doing well for yourself physically, emotionally, and spiritually can benefit a great many others when the bounty of your energy and merit of your actions are extended to others. Start with yourself and the relationships closest to you, bonding with people who resonate with your energy, and releasing relationships that are toxic, drain your energy, or feel discouraging. Associate with people who respect you and support your lifestyle and goals for happiness. Your efforts to be happy and extend happiness to others are like putting pebbles into the center of a very large pond, ripples extending outward toward the shore affecting the entirety of the water body including everybody and everything in it. The ripple effect will be felt more strongly by the people closest to you, and to your relief and surprise will even float some people and situations farther away from you. The more consciously you put pebbles into the pond, you will be affecting positive change to the world on a regular basis.

An ideal outcome of a spiritual crisis is awakening, which arises out of healing from crisis. An ideal outcome of awakening is clarity, which arises from yoga, mindfulness, and meditation as I have suggested, or other healing integration practices. An ideal outcome of having clarity is a realization or vision of what you might be able to accomplish with your natural gifts, skills, and talents. No matter what your background or origin, we all share the same basic desire to be healthy, happy, and whole. I haven't met a single person who says they aren't striving for these goals, even if they have no idea how to do that or where to begin. Your work is one of the first places to look when you are wondering how you contribute to a better world, and this applies to any job you do in or out of the home, paid or unpaid. Ask yourself these questions:

1. Can I use my special senses or abilities in the job I currently do? Is it possible for me to use my gifts to enhance my productivity, improve communication between people or departments, or to make my job more enjoyable?
2. Do I feel respected and valued at work?
3. Do I get internal satisfaction from the job I do?
4. Would I be happier if I changed my work environment? Would I benefit from changing where I do my work, such as working from home instead of an office, or in a different department?
5. Would I be happier if I did a different kind of job? Would

I be happier if I worked alone, set my own goals, made my own product or service, or work with a company I endorse and respect?

6. What do I feel passionate about? What change do I want to see in the world, and am I contributing to that in the job I do?

Change my career? Change my life? Change the world?

Consider where you are in the healing process, and how well equipped you feel to endure a major change in your life. Consider your passions. Who do you wish to serve? Consider your abilities. What do you wish to create? Consider your connections to like-minded people and organizations. Whom do you wish to connect with? Finding a mentor or a coach can help you identify some answers to these questions and guide you toward achieving reasonable goals that will give you satisfaction and contentment. Have patience and faith that the healing and growth process will lead you towards opportunities for learning and meeting the right individuals who may play a role in what you do next.

There is much to be learned through the yoga experience itself—the union and connection with God or spirit that provides the path to healing is the same union that will guide your purpose. If your healing was facilitated by a spiritual counselor or a team of healing arts professionals, those relationships will continue to guide you toward your higher purpose. The energy that awakens you to the Oneness of all Things will eventually guide you to serving, creating, educating, or guiding the process for others. When you have reduced your suffering and healed yourself, you have nothing but a great privilege to continue on, connecting people, creating healing experiences for others, contributing to the wholeness and peacefulness of humanity. One of yoga's highest merits is serving and guiding others towards a happier life.

If the CEOs of the world's largest companies were to grow a

healthy, people-centered, environmentally conscious business, how much different would our world look? If every single person followed their heart and put action behind their compassion, how much greater would our impact in the world be? If every parent, partner, and caretaker were healed of their own hurts and anger, how much better would their relationships be? Hurt people hurt people, so it is imperative that the people who have healed themselves continue to be an example of love and compassion to others. Highly sensitive people have an important place in this world to lead companies that stand up for the wellbeing of the Earth and its inhabitants.

If I were a Manager for XYZ Widget Corporation instead of teaching yoga, I am certain that my spiritual path would still lead me to want to create a happy work environment for my employees. Since running a large business for big profit is not usually people-centered, I know I'm not the best person for that job. I would likely be distracted from the company's bottom line by tending to the needs of the team, so my only interest in business is to train business leaders to put the earth and people as top priority when designing their products and manufacturing processes. If independent healers can help business leaders awaken to the needs of the planet, I am confident that more people-centered, environmentally friendly business will emerge.

What we do for a living is less important than how we make an impact doing it based on our standards and priorities when looking for a job, accepting a job, and doing that job. As a mechanic, my priority would be to make an honest repair, and build positive customer relationships. As a stay-at-home parent, my highest priority would be to build positive relationships by fostering love and respect in the home. The freedom to care about and serve an individual or group of individuals becomes limited in a large organization, but I am hopeful that this will change as more business leaders change their priorities from a money-driven mission to a people and environment focused mission. It is each person's responsibility to find the best way to serve their family, community, or the world with their skills and passions, whether that is with a small group or a large company. As we awaken to higher purpose, we can awaken to better ways of working, living, and enjoying life and the shift is happening now. Many old ways of thinking and doing business have shifted for the better, but more progressive, influential, and sensitive people are needed in leadership positions to continue this progress. As an example, anti-smoking laws have become more stringent in favor of public health in regards to smoking, the same has not happened yet with food or wellness practices outside of the medical establishment. Perhaps technology will be the tool that enables highly sensitive people to work for large companies and influence the way business is done to benefit humans, animals, and the environment.

Your purpose will be made apparent to you when you remain connected to the healing source, because that healing source is the source of all of us. What you actually do to make a living with that purpose in mind is up to you. The key is maintaining connections shared among people, the experience of humanity coming into wholeness and your service toward the betterment of the whole. It is up to each person to decide how to best serve the greater good, and everyone has their own unique talents and natural abilities. Serving your world can be done locally and individually, or in groups and organizations—there is no limit to what your life can be like when you serve your higher purpose.

Meditate on what you do considerably well—and enjoy—then take a look at opportunities to use your natural abilities. There will always be suffering people in the world who will seek relief in the form of a product or service, and someone needs to be available in their community who will provide it. Every community needs builders, fixers, farmers, healers, educators, and artists. For every person who has a body, a mind, and a spirit, they each need a home, healthy food, a job, task, or vocation according to their ability, a healer for when they are sick, sad, or hurt, sources of knowledge and education, and people to beautify and inspire us to enjoy our environment. If each healer, farmer, builder, educator, and artist used materials and resources that did not harm the environment or other humans, each person awakening to their highest and best purpose, think of how much better our world would be! Use what you know or look into trainings that build on your natural talents such as technical, musical, linguistic, and business. Knowledge and experience can always be acquired but there is no substitute for innate ability and enjoying what you do. Take time to discover what your heart really wants to accomplish in this life, and then take a step toward doing it.

If you have no idea what you do well, ask a family member or friend, or consider what you enjoy doing most and find an environmentally responsible and humanistic way to do it. And do not dismiss responses that compliment your interpersonal skills such as, "You listen to me really well" or "You give me comfort." People who listen deeply and really care are of great value to every community because all commercial enterprise and human services are based on solving someone else's problem or filling a need. Great listeners are needed in all vocations because you can only fix, sell, or create something according to someone's needs when you know through all of your senses what is needed to solve the problem.

There is really no requirement that you change your career or job on your quest for higher purpose, but you may feel deep inside that it must be done. How you earn your livelihood or contribute to your family is related to your personal values, which may change as you change. This is a part of realizing how you as an individual are a part of a greater interconnected web and that you contribute to or detract from the wellbeing of the planet, fellow humans, and animals. A change in your values may require a change in your approach to doing your current job, or it may mean changing your vocation entirely. The goal is to follow your higher purpose while staying connected to health, healing, and wholeness. For you this may mean transitioning to a smaller eco-conscious employer that really takes care and consideration toward its employees. You might be inspired to start your very own company, provide a valuable, compassionate service, or even learn how to become a professional healer or teacher. You may prefer to care for children or the elderly, create art or a community garden. The point is to strive toward connecting to the highest good of all living things, no matter how small, and no matter how long it takes. Don't worry about how long it will take to achieve something; the time will pass anyways, so make each day an opportunity to connect to your highest and best purpose. Once you are on your quest, nothing can stop you!

One can live a perfectly decent life without knowing precisely any other purpose they are here on earth to serve. I must add that there is nothing wrong with a person who doesn't claim to have a higher purpose, so we needn't judge anyone. But this question runs in the background of nearly everyone's mind sooner or later, whether or not they act upon it, and it is up to each individual to determine if they wish to discover what that is, and then decide whether it is worth trying to achieve it. There are certainly some personal and political circumstances in the world that would nearly prohibit a person's inquiry of their higher purpose, but there are many true stories of individuals who overcame terrible abuse and oppression to achieve greater personal, spiritual, and financial freedom. Individual determination is a powerful thing, but judging someone else for their old-fashioned, unenlightened views and actions is a sadder thing.

When the light dawns on us, an unfortunate shadow is cast over others who do not believe the way we do, or who are not open to changing their ways as we did. When I was going through this process I justified my judgmental beliefs, and reasoned that it was because I knew better now that I could look down on people who did things that I did in the not-so-distant past. Over time I grew weary—and a little guilty—over feeling judgmental of others for their ignorance, especially because I could start to see the fallibility of my own thoughts and behaviors! As my awareness increased, disdain for my fellow humans grew in intensity and I realized that judging others was not a part of my life's purpose, and I had to stop. Being judgmental was quite the opposite of my purpose! Judging and labeling people is a way to disconnect and separate people from each other, and that was against my purpose of practicing yoga off the mat by finding common ground and connection. I could finally see how I had been participating in a cycle of suffering by judging or criticizing others, a trait which I then wanted to change.

My yoga and meditation practice led me to an awareness of my propensity to judge others, which led me to see the opposite: my deeper desire to have harmony and peace. Yoga is finding a balance between the opposites, so I needed to apply an opposing vision to my meditation to generate compassion. Rather than seeing people who made selfish or harmful choices as "stupid," I saw the truth that every person including myself is ignorant of many things outside their scope of understanding. A limited view obscures good choices and produces behavior that is not always in the best interests of humanity. When people serve narrow interests, or are desperate to fill basic needs such as food, shelter, physical or emotional safety, or love, they are generally not concerned with serving a higher purpose because their very human needs are not being met. This is like the butterfly who cannot recall that it had been a caterpillar larvae just days ago.

My next meditation endeavor was to learn to generate compassion for everyone regardless of their views. It doesn't mean that I accepted everything under the sun and just went along with things that were contrary to my beliefs. I did a lot of reflective meditation to discern what kinds of relationships I felt would be most beneficial for me, and what kind of business I wanted to build that would achieve my higher purpose. I wanted to bridge the gap between the spiritual and human experience through compassion and healing arts. And nothing has been more important to me in my work than deepening this connection with others through compassion.

This transformation was the beginning of my becoming a healer: first as a touch healer, and later as an energy healer and yoga educator. When I became a deep listener with all of my senses, I was able to get to the root of people's problems and guide my clients appropriately according to their needs, instead of just giving them a band-aid. I am interested in helping people pull out the roots of their problems, not just tending the weeds!

If you're not clear about your higher purpose, you may feel burdened or pressured to do something different based on achieving that purpose. Let it unfold in due time—there is no need to rush it. Listen to guidance. If it comes on suddenly, you could feel burdened or crushed by this knowledge because now you have to change something, but you can embrace changes a little at a time. It really is a choice, but you'll know when you are living according to your true self or not. The power of awareness and awakening is also the power to decide what to do with it!

Spiritual awareness is like having a super power but I caution against identifying with the super hero who makes the crisis their purpose for living. Awakening is a gate through which you pass by deliberate action or being thrust through it, like a superhero, who endures a catastrophe or tragedy in their life, but the super hero does not ever heal from the crisis. The sad and gifted super hero embraces a false identity to covers their wounds, but never heals them. They suffer in solitude, endlessly searching for justice and retribution, but most never heal, find a tribe, or empower others to heal.

Even if you are the only person you know who has experienced a spiritual crisis or awakening, many people have and still are moving through their own awakenings as you are, and it is best to find them. Meditating and healing from the events that may have caused you to experience crisis can help you see that you are not the lone super hero and you are not made up of the events and circumstances that have happened to you. When you do get the chance to share what has happened to you, note how you relate to the events or experiences in your life or relationships from the past—do you call them your own with personal pronouns such as *my* diabetes, *my* anxiety, *my* insomnia, or *my* ex? Do you know someone who talks about "*their* accident" or "*their* depression" that seems to be the cause of all their suffering? The way we view our circumstances is directly related to how we heal from those circumstances, so word choice is important.

When you talk about the circumstances or people that have caused you harm or sadness, avoid referring to them as yours because you are identifying with the very thing you wish would stop harming you. If it happened in the past, let it be there in the past. Consider the labels you use to describe conditions and relationships: some may be temporary no matter how long they have been present in your life, and some may have been given to you by a person in authority.

As an example, if you say, "*My* depression came on because of all *my* migraines after *my* accident last year," tells your subconscious that these are permanent conditions occurring in the present moment. The truth would still be told if it was reframed as, "I have been experiencing a lot of pressure and pain in my head since I was in a bad accident last year, and this has caused me to feel sad and lonely." Both statements are clear and truthful but the second talks about how you have been feeling, which leaves space in the mind for a change in the experience. In the mind, our feelings and our description of an experience can change, but an identifying label cannot. Always leave room for your experience to change.

On your quest for higher purpose, awakening to spiritual truths can also feel awfully lonely. Awakening is both a blessing and a curse, and it can cause you to behave reactively. You can use your gifts for good or let the magnitude of possibility weigh you down. It really is a blessing when you get through the awkwardness of being different, because you will have greater insight into your higher purpose and how to achieve it. It also feels like a curse because you will feel awkward and strange around others for a while, and you will be full of frustration that either everyone is delusional or that you are going a little crazy. You may even feel guilty or mean for thinking and saying things that make you appear self-righteous. You are really just speaking the truth, and the truth is hard to take for many people.

There is no right or wrong way to open to Spirit, and you can't plan for enlightenment. It doesn't matter whether you're six or 86, but it can happen when you decide to be still and mindful. No matter how it starts for you, young or old or in between, if you settle down for a time, as I did with my empty six-year-old mind, I believe it can happen for you. Perhaps you have already had an awakening to Spirit? Perhaps you have felt that tingling of truth and rightness, but thought it was just a chill? Perhaps you were discouraged from exploring that experience because someone told you it was false or weird? There is no better time to revisit that feeling and connect with All that Is. Time is all we have here. Realizing you want harmony and peace in your life is the foundation for creating what you want, which is harmony with your family and community, with vast ripples of compassion spreading out into the world. At our heart, we all want that. Living your highest purpose with more embracement, more unity, more love, and more compassion is a great privilege we should not squander.

14

I KNOW WHAT I FEEL: BLANCA'S JOURNEY

As a child, I could sense things and see people who were not in their body. No-one in my family gave me guidance, and I did not have any early training in how to understand or work with these gifts. I became afraid and so I disregarded and buried my senses as best I could, but I could never completely turn them off. I always had a curiosity about reincarnation, spirits, hauntings, and life after death and the supernatural. I felt guilty that I was offending God as I fed my curiosity when I would watch TV shows or read about spiritual topics in secret. Being in a Catholic family, I struggled with why God would consider my natural talents as bad or evil, but these messages of sacrilege were ever-present in my life where church dogma and faith were paramount in my home.

I lived in a state of crisis for the first 30 years of my life. Although I was loved by my immediate family, I lived with a very poor self-image, self-hatred, and I endured great physical and mental pain due to trauma and abuse from extended family members. My earliest support came from my mother and my aunt who loved me dearly, but my mother passed away when I was only 15. My aunt knew about the abuse I had endured and worked in her own way to bring healing to me which I hold in my heart and mind to this day. For most of my life I have lived with migraines, pain, and constant worry. Living with supernatural, paranormal senses is not an easy way to live, but the abuse compounded my difficulties into my adult years. The childhood trauma in my past led to several complex medical diagnoses in adulthood, and I eventually accepted pharmaceutical interventions which was helpful at the time to quiet my mind. I was more productive in my work and spent less time worrying; however, I was not getting to the root of the issues I wrestled with and I was determined to reduce my dependency on mood stabilizers.

I tried to take care of myself through prayer, counseling, exercise, biofeedback, and massage, but these were temporary and did not give me the lasting peace that I sought. I eventually left full-time work to dedicate more time to healing and recovery. I returned to school to study massage. During massage class, I learned about different alternative healing modalities. One day a Shaman spoke to us in class and I began working with her privately. I experienced a significant breakthrough when I traveled to Peru to work with plant medicine healers, and at the age of 49 I finally began to feel freedom from the emotions that had plagued me most of my life. I have since learned to do energy healing such as reiki and I receive treatments and counseling in Spiritual Response Therapy.

One complication I experienced when healing with spiritual energies is that I was born and raised to practice Catholicism. I attended all the required religion classes as a child and received all the sacraments of the church, but I felt a profound guilt and shame that I had offended God or disappointed the church and my family when I did my spiritual work or connected with God in a way that was different than the church's way. For a long time, I could not even look at the face of God in church because of shame. It took me many years to reconcile how I wanted to live my faith. Today, I believe in God —Father, Son, Holy Spirit —but I do not believe in hell. I believe that there is a way that our souls are reconciled for those errors which have hurt the souls around us. I believe that in the end we will all be together with God. The God I believe in does not want his people to live eternally in hell. The God I believe in is a loving God who wants all his people to live together with him in Joy.

I am still on my healing journey, but I now see my gifts in a different light. Today I see my gifts as gifts from God. My special senses and gifts of awakening help me daily. I strive not to judge people, but rather to support them in their journey towards healing. I ask for God's strength, love, and guidance when I counsel people in positive ways to help them move forward. I am a positive person who prays not only for my own healing but for the healing of those I love and all the people of the world.

15

SELF-CARE AND THE DO-LESS LIST

ALL NECESSARY THINGS

When I am hungry, I eat, and when thirsty I drink.
Not too much, not too little,
Balancing what I need with what I do not.
When tired, I rest.
I have all that I need, and do not take, crave,
nor covet what I do not.
I know what is in me, and what is not.
My feelings are mine, but I do not own them
And they do not own me.
Your feelings are not mine,
They are your experience and belong to you
while they are with you.
But they do not own you, nor me, nor any other.
The weather is here, and is necessary for nature's continuance,
But you cannot hold the weather, nor control it.
I sit and sip my tea, watching it all pass by like the weather.

Empathy is one of the most commonly shared experiences among highly sensitive people. Feeling the energy of other people all the time can make a person feel anxious, isolated, and vulnerable. An empath soaks up the emotional landscape like a sponge and feels weighed down by sadness, frustration, and disappointment, or elated with happiness and optimism, depending on who they surround themselves with. Empaths unintentionally amplify their suffering, because they are unable to distinguish between their own emotions and those generated from the source. When surrounded by crowds it can be nearly impossible to find out who is the source of negative energy, and when alone at home, a highly sensitive person can be affected even by the emotions of people on the radio or television. In the life of an empath, even grocery shopping or birthday parties can be daunting.

When an empath takes care to surround themselves with positivity and optimism, they are likely to feel more of that, but if they are around too many people at once or people who have strong negative energy, they will feel that, too. An empath feels the feelings of others without discernment between which are their own feelings and which are absorbed into them. The problem is not that they feel too much; it is that they may be confused about how to handle the sensations and feelings that threaten to overwhelm them. Energy management specialists are emerging in this growing tribe of empaths and highly sensitive people who are teaching others energy management strategies, techniques, and life-hacks that create healthy boundaries so empaths can work and play. If something causes a person pain or suffering, it is beneficial for that person to learn how to insulate themselves better and to generate and preserve their own energy for their own use. Empathy is like a super-power: it is a gift that comes with some drawbacks, with potential for great power and responsibility.

The problem with empathy is not in the feeling itself; dysfunctional empathy is caused by a lack of control over the push and pull of their emotions, and a sense of helplessness in trying to moderate their feelings. The outpourings of an unaware empath can sound like pleading soundbites from non-profit infomercials on late-night television to 'Save the Children' or 'Sponsor-a-Starving-Puppy'. A highly sensitive person with no control over their emotions is over-whelmed at the suffering of the world as well as their limited ability to address any of it. There can be a lot of crying and frustration in the life of a highly-sensitive person, and they often feel desperate for relief because the suffering of the world is too much to bear. An empath can identify with the Buddhist deity Avalokiteshvara, the Compassionate One who "hears the cries of the world."

Even if you are not a true empath by definition, feeling a lot of sensory information, emotion, and creative thoughts can interfere with your ability to maintain a peaceful life. Maybe you just want to slow down to enjoy what you feel is important in life, and do less of what you feel is less important. It's not necessary to label yourself an empath; just knowing you are a highly sensitive per-son is enough to justify making changes to preserve your energy and peace of mind. You don't need a diagnosis or permission from anyone to insulate your life a little more. You can take extra quiet time and self-care measures to have a healthy, happy life without adopting a label or explaining to anyone why you chose to do so. Once you know what and how you feel, mindfulness practice can help you to stay aware of when you are picking up on the emotions of others or extra-sensory information.

Be aware of how you feel when you are around certain people or in certain environments. If you want to slow the flow of informa-tion and sensation, it is wise to avoid situations that overstimulate you or make you feel uncomfortable. It's not fair to you to double your suffering by taking on an emotional burden that isn't yours to begin with. Absorbing other people's problems doesn't actually relieve anyone else of their problems—it actually doubles the suf-fering. Simplify your life so that you are more comfortable in your regular environment, with plenty of time to rest and recuperate between obligations and encounters with people outside of that environment or with people who negatively affect your energy. Reducing the frequency of encounters with negative stimulations is really a matter of self-preservation and self-care in order to focus yourself on quality information and quality time in peace. Consider spending less time in the company of anyone or in any environment that depletes your energy and adopt more self-care measures that will make you an agent of healing and transformation.

One Zen student said, "My teacher is the best. He can go days without eating." The second said, "My teacher has so much self-control, he can go days without sleep." The third said, "My teacher is so wise that he eats when he's hungry and sleeps when he's tired."

~ Zen Buddhist joke

Highly sensitive people feel overwhelmed because they cannot filter all the information they receive, and they may lack coping strategies such as energy management skills to help manage the input. Like a computer with factory storage capacity, our minds can get bogged down with too much information which makes them slow down or even crash when downloading a very large file. Our thinking can get slow, confused, and even freeze up from time to time when the flow of spiritual or sensory information exceeds our capacity to process it. This is a cue to slow down to filter it and digest it. Quite simply, resist the urge to press on at normal speed. Eat when you're hungry, sleep when you're tired, and take extra time to process.

Consider how busy you are in your daily life. How much activity is really necessary? How can you create more space in your life to get the quiet healing time you need? Are there some things you can do less of to create more space for healing? These are important questions in the life of a highly sensitive person. Busy-ness is too often encouraged and excessively glorified in modern cultures that make everything a box to be checked off at the end of the day.

Busy-ness is one way to guarantee you won't acknowledge your need to be angry, sad, disgusted, annoyed or in grief. Staying overly-busy means you don't have time to think about how you feel or what may be coming from other sources. Busy-ness can be a coping mechanism designed to keep control of day to day activities, so that no one is inconvenienced by the downtime of dealing with heavy emotions. If you put great pressure on yourself to be available for others, sidelining your own self-care, please don't. Putting yourself last just delays your healing time and may result in a serious lack of creative energy and can also have serious physical side-effects such as illness, fatigue, and depression. Do not exclude yourself from the very prescription of self-care you would want your loved ones to observe. Delaying or not acknowledging your own need to heal and recover is denying your emotional and physical well-being.

Does self-care sound like one big task on top of your already busy life? Be wary that in the wrong mindset, even self-care can become a thing to check off your to-do list, leaving you feeling rushed or strained, crowded in by the tasks that have somehow taken over your life and become obligations. Consider scheduling self-care on your calendar to make sure you have time for yourself, but resist making self-care just another box to check off at the end of the day. Stay mindful of your daily routines and reduce or eliminate unnecessary tasks to prioritize healing and recuperation time as a part of your normal, happy life!

Massage and yoga and taking long walks on the beach sound like such a wonderful way to live, so the question is why do so many people avoid it? Why in the world would someone decide to stick their head in the sand and not deal with their emotional well-being? Well, because emotions are hard to deal with, and not everyone is comfortable taking care of themselves. There can be a lot of guilt and shame from old programming wrapped up with any effort to do something loving for them. Feelings are sticky, icky, and have associated memories and physiological stuff mixed up with them. Crying can bring on a headache for some people due to pressure in the head area and increased sinus activity. Anger can make us feel tense and hot inside. Fear and anxiety can make us feel nauseous or short of breath. Healing is not for the weak—it can actually be hard work, and that's why having a support professional is a good idea to help you process whatever comes up during the process. Remember that the nature of feelings is that they always change. Feelings are temporary. Be patient in your practice to recognize that you are not your feelings, and that your feelings do not own you.

Are peace and harmony your favorite choices for conflict resolution? The dysfunctional side of peace and harmony is called, "sweeping it under the rug," or "making nice-nice." As a peace-loving person, dismissing your emotions may seem like a nice solution, but speaking up for yourself in a tactful and meaningful way is a more positive way of expressing how you feel without damaging someone else. Anger is an especially difficult emotion for someone on the spiritual path, primarily because they think they shouldn't ever be angry with someone. It would be so nice if compassion could immediately rise up to greet anger with a big hug and soothe it all out! No matter how extreme your feelings are, all feelings are real and valid, even if you know intellectually that they are not permanent. Look into what your feelings are trying to teach you, and do not dismiss or criticize yourself for feeling them.

I used to be the master of dismissed and denied emotions. I used to deny, over-schedule, over-do and cover it all up with activity to avoid intense feelings. Projects, parties, classes, cleaning—you name it. But eventually the project ends, the party's over, the class stops, and the cleaning is endless. What's next? How about not doing anything for a day? An hour? Five minutes? How long would it take to have your real feelings come forth and express themselves? How long would it take for you to sit with them, feel them, and accept how you feel? It's about as long as the time it takes to learn how to be truly mindful.

When I was teaching myself how to meditate, it took me about 20 minutes of forced stillness, and then the tears welled up and spilled over. I recognized for once in a very long time how I felt: guilty, sad, and lost. Although I felt strongly about one day achieving my goals and dreams, I also felt plagued with self-doubt, judgement, and criticism about myself and others. On a scale of 1–10, with a 1 being unable to get out of bed and a 10 being vibrant wellbeing, at my lowest point I was functioning at a 3.

I had to work through a lot of anger and sadness with words that I really did not want anyone else to hear, so I started journaling and writing poetry. Through my art, poetry, and writing, I could see and feel that I was at least two different people in the same body: peaceful, loving, and silly on the one hand, and angry and wounded on the other, which was causing a lot of disharmony within me. I worked out my feelings over time with writing, energywork, yoga, and counseling, and started spending more time in quiet reflection which I have maintained to this day.

I often remind my students to take great interest in their own self-care daily by bringing attention to their practice and "filling your own cup first." To fill your own cup means to replenish your internal resources regularly. The phrase, "My cup runneth over," comes from the Hebrew Psalm 23:5 meaning that you have more than enough for your needs, which takes some intent and dedication to assure that you do. It does not happen by itself. When you have sufficient attention, love, health, and energy, you will naturally have plenty of those things to give to children, family, work, and creative pursuits, but you cannot give what you do not have. Depleting your own personal resources will not serve you or your family in the long run. Filling your own cup, giving daily attention to your breath, your body, and your emotional state is an absolute necessity.

An overflowing cup of vitality is full of the necessary things you need to quench your thirst, to satiate your hunger, and nourish you well emotionally and physically. If your cup "runneth over," you might say you are at a 9 or 10. On the scale of 1–10 mentioned above, how well do you feel? If you are not feeling that well now, recall a time in your life that you felt near a 9 or 10—what's happened since then to draw your energy down to a 4 or below? Was it a slow decline, or one single event? Without going into detail or placing blame, you may be able to see clearly with a little mindful attention the path toward establishing a steady increase of vitality.

At the beginning of each of my yoga training groups, I give a 10-Day Health Journal assignment. I ask that each student track 10 consecutive days of what they eat or ingest, how much and what kind of exercise, how many hours of sleep and the quality of sleep, and how they manage their stress. In addition to seeing their habits for what they truly are, students also discover how often they judge themselves for not doing what they know they "should." Before they even start the assignment, I tell them that even more importantly than the benefits they will see in their long-term health, is their honesty with themselves about their experience. Sharing that experience in the group is optional, but an important step in having accountability for the changes you wish to make. One thing is for certain: we cannot change what we don't acknowledge or face. We begin by learning to detach from judgement and criticism right at the start, even as we start to make small changes. At the end of the 10 days, everyone has loosened up a bit on how they view their habits: they are habits, which are mostly unconscious or culturally ingrained. With a little mindfulness, they can begin to see how their habits developed and which need to change. They all admit it is far better to be honest with themselves even if they don't know right away how to change what they eat, when they go to bed, or how to be more active when they are at work, or react to stress differently. That's part of what they hope to learn from being in the program. Small changes start with awareness of how the habit came into being, whether they are still serving you well or not, and one thing with which to replace that habit.

In addition to caring for yourself, what if you take care of other people as a part of your normal routine? If you are responsible for providing caregiving for children or parents, or healthcare to clients or students, you are someone who is constantly offering to others whatever is in that cup of yours. If everyone keeps sipping at that cup and you do not have the support or resources to refill it, it will go dry, crack, and certainly break over time. And if you have been through—or are going through—a spiritual crisis, the deterioration will occur much faster, simply because the process of awakening requires your attention. The downloading of information will continue, and you must be mentally present to digest and assimilate it.

This is why I feel that having a regular yoga and mindfulness practice is essential for self-care and healing. Yoga asks us to bring attention to our bodies, to give them care with no harm and no judgement. We listen to the small voice inside that deserves to be heard. We get out of thinking mode and into feeling mode to develop insight and wisdom into our true nature. An appropriate yoga practice sustained over time will provide you with the attention to your body and mind necessary to refuel your internal resources. Giving regular attention to your mind and body builds a trusting relationship within yourself, and this can go a long way toward filling your cup.

Consider sharing your journey with your family by being as open and honest with them that you intend to make some changes to your time or task management. Hear yourself sharing what you need for balance in your life. Give your reasons so they know that the outcome is intended to help you be a happier and healthier person which they will benefit from. But be prepared that not everyone may be comfortable with that level of transparency, nor is it your responsibility to make them comfortable. It does not mean you are not compassionate or loving if you put yourself first in some things. I assure you that taking care of yourself will put you in a much better position to help take care of others—when you are well—so take care of yourself by choice, not because you're last on the list.

Take a little time to ask yourself each day, "how do I feel?" The answer to that question may not always be easy, but it is the start of a beautiful relationship —with yourself. Take a moment during mindful breathing to ask yourself that question as you would a close friend. Kindle a true friendship with yourself so that you can be honest with how you feel. Adding this to your daily practice will build trust inside of you that what you feel is true and correct for you, awakening a little more understanding and inner peace. It is this deep listening within yourself that can eventually guide you toward greater wisdom.

Many people have resistance to this movement of taking care of oneself first; that it is selfish and gratuitous to spend so much time navel-gazing. When push comes to shove and your plane is going down, so to speak, the flight attendants show you how to put on your own oxygen mask before helping children and others with theirs. If your family is not the place you will receive the understanding, patience, and support you desire, you may need to find support elsewhere in your local area or online community. Spiritual or religious centers can provide respite and guidance for spiritual matters, and organized group classes and support groups can be found under the names of yoga centers, healing arts centers, community centers, and wellness centers.

One of the most common symptoms of stress that has gone on far too long is anxiety. There is a lot of scientific support for taking care of yourself to avoid many preventable health and emotional problems. According to Harvard Health Publications, nearly two-thirds of the estimated 57 million adults with anxiety disorders are women. What people afflicted by these disorders have in common is persistent, irrational fear or distress that interferes with daily life. Anxiety is strongly related to the onset of physical symptoms such as pain, nausea, weakness, or dizziness that have no apparent physiologic cause. This means that chronic stress and anxiety often precedes physical illnesses including heart disease, respiratory problems such as shortness of breath, and gastrointestinal conditions such as constipation, bloating, and ulcers. For those who put off receiving care for either issue, the physical symptoms often become worse. The Harvard University Women's Health Team suggests relaxation techniques such as stretching and walking as a part of a self-care regimen. It just makes good sense to take care of one's own health and wellbeing before, and on an ongoing basis, when taking care of others. And this goes double for people in care-taking and teaching roles. Filling your own cup first is in no way a selfish act.

Christina Grof, coauthor of *The Stormy Search for the Self* tells how she started to focus more on her own self-care with a "Want to Do" list that transformed her feelings of obligation into activities of joy. "When darkness descends, joy is blotted out, buried, seemingly non-existent. Everything weighed like a heavy burden, all my activities felt like obligations. When I realized that I had forgotten joy, I created a "want-to-do" list. Every time I found myself wandering around in a fog, my job was to pull out the list and do something enjoyable or productive. I organized closets and took walks, finally starting to see the beauty around me. And I focused on others – being a good friend, showing up for someone in need. My self-care didn't suffer. My diet stayed healthy, and I kept up with yoga. But some people going through hard times can benefit from paying special attention to the basics of daily living with a good diet, exercise, and limited alcohol."

In an effort to love yourself more, you sometimes need to do less, lighten your load, and free yourself up to enJOY your life. Here is my full permission to enJOY life by doing LESS:

The Do-LESS List

1. Do less housecleaning. Housecleaning is the #1 reported obstacle to having quiet time for self-care at home. If you can just stop concerning yourself with dust bunnies or things to put away or clean, you will have gifted yourself up to several free hours to have the healing quiet time you need. Making your bed is the #2 thing people decided to stop doing. Although it may be unsightly, it is an example of allowing something to be untidy that does not harm anyone or anything. Doing less frivolous or purposeless activity even for a month will afford you extra time you never knew you had. Make the perfect cup of tea and sit in your favorite chair before you do anything else that day.

2. Watch less TV. When I asked my clients for a short list of things that they should immediately stop doing to have less stress, the #3 wasteful activity was watching TV—especially the news. Non-stop media is an empath's nightmare. TV and social media are designed to hook your emotions with images and stories and gossip. If you must check the news, set a time limit such as 5 minutes per day to get the top stories, and then turn it off. Up the ante to checking the news just once or twice a week and you will discover a whole new perspective on life sans terror, sadness, and political tug of war.

3. Do less worrying. No, *stop* worrying, because the past is in the past and the future has not happened yet. Meditate daily and you will burn any desire to worry out of your system. You will have clarity on future plans, and release attachment to things you cannot control. A version of the serenity prayer and affirmation works well here: "God/Divine Power, I accept serenity for the things I cannot change, courage to change the things I can, and wisdom to know the difference."

4. Do less small talk. Postpone going to parties or gatherings while you are in healing. Small talk can be boring, easily turns into gossip, and saps your precious energy. Small gestures mean

a lot when you consider sending a handwritten card or call on the phone instead if you decide not to attend an event. Learn to say, "No thank you" to things that are not absolutely necessary or contribute to your well-being. People will still love you and appreciate that you are taking the time to heal, especially when you have found the right balance of internal peace with external socializing.

5. Do less work. Or change how you do work so that it feels more like play. Attract the things that bring you joy—music, art, and friendly, supportive co-workers. If your work is not that sort of place, consider what kind of job would feel rewarding to you. No need to make changes now, but the time may be coming soon when you require a more rewarding environment. Don't take on new or unnecessary projects. Make a short list to store your most important ideas during your healing and integration process. Wait or delegate until you have good health and a positive mindset to move forward with any project.

Holding onto things can also be a source of stress, so you may need to lose some baggage. Holding onto heavy luggage doesn't make for a smooth journey; it bogs you down, and causes a lot of distraction from important internal work in your meditation. You don't want to hurt anyone's feelings by getting rid of your favorite collectibles, but receiving more also feels more like a burden than the sentiment with which the gift was intended. There comes a time in your life when more stuff doesn't equal happiness and more tangible stuff, even gifts, create more stress than joy. It's not that you're ungrateful—quite the contrary! When your heart opens up to the beauty and generosity of this world, you appreciate nearly everything! You're so darned grateful that you want to give proper respect for absolutely everything that has ever been given to you like children's artwork, knick-knacks from vacationing friends, handcrafted do-dads, and store-bought things your well-meaning partner gave you to make your life easier or your home more beautiful.

But it's okay to admit that clutter causes stress. The more stuff you have to handle, store, clean, or dispose of, there is indeed a burden that wasn't there before. Tangible objects occupy space, and that space is your sacred environment. What is in your sacred environment? How much control do you have over the things that come into your sacred space? Your home environment and your body is a temple. Highly sensitive people need to take special care of the ingredients that go into food, body care, and clothing because they come into the body itself, affecting how we feel. If we are lucky, we breath clean air and drink clean water, but what we buy and bring into our home and workplace is often created someplace else, and that will affect our health. The raw materials that create everything from body care products to home appliances actually come from all over the world. Unless we make it ourselves, our knowledge of the raw materials and manufacturing that goes into the creation, packaging, use, and disposal of the product when its usability has come to an end is also limited. But we can buy and use less. Gifts and products —let's call it "stuff" —are all things that occupy finite space. If only we could send it all to the iCloud! The stress accumulates when we get overwhelmed with the task of appropriating each item to its most respectable, earth-friendly, or benevolent destination. When we reach a threshold of accumulation, we try to make a responsible choice to give it away or throw it away. All of that redistribution of stuff takes valuable time away from things we'd much rather be doing, like sipping tea or watching trees.

I had my own transition with collectibles, and decided to work a plan so that my family would understand my change in preferences. The things I had accumulated caused me such distress that I wanted to find out how Buddhist teachers and minimalists handle receiving gifts, because they choose not to accumulate anything beyond what they can use in the present. I figured the monk, of all people, would know the most tactful and gracious way to do away with things they cannot own or choose not to keep. I studied the gift-receiving habits of Tibetan Buddhist lamas, and discovered that they are the most efficient re-gifters in history! Keep in mind that someone like His Holiness the Dalai Lama has a literal posse of people who control how a gift is received, so they don't get a lot of stuffed animals or items of clothing like a pop star. But what they do receive is redistributed to someone who can use it right away. Also, minimalists are not shy about sharing their simplistic lifestyle, and they help family and friends understand why meaningful experiences are of more value to them than presents. Over a period of a couple of years, I was able to successfully communicate with my family that consumables and activity gifts were the best kinds of gifts for me. This win-win situation meant more health-related gifts, and fun, exciting new adventures shared with me by my loved ones, and far fewer messy shelving units full of things to dust and clean.

Buying less stuff and getting less stuff can go a long way towards lightening your sacred space in your home. What about doing less? What can you stop doing *today* that will afford you the quiet healing time you need and deserve? Even small changes can help you loosen up areas of your life that have been constricting your personal, spiritual, or creative energy. Don't be afraid to do LESS so that in the future you can enJOY MORE.

The Do MORE Self-Care List
1. Do more yoga. The basics of yoga can be learned from books, videos, or community classes. You can start with the breathing exercises in this book, and add some stretches as you feel able. Social media, when used appropriately, can also be helpful in finding a local teacher or yoga therapist in your area who can help you learn an appropriate method of yoga that is right for you.
2. Get more healing touch. I once heard a dance teacher sing a cute little ditty to remind the parents of her students that

children need, "three hugs a day, that's the minimum, three hugs a day, not the maximum, three hugs a day, to let them know they're loved!" Hugs and hand holding are a simply wonderful healing comfort. If you are able, get a massage or a reiki energy treatment which are forms of professional healing touch, sometimes available at low cost, barter, or trade.

3. Spend more time in nature. When you get your feet on the grass and your face in the sun, good things happen. Brain chemistry improves, mood improves, and you create and activate vitamin D3 from the sun. People who spend more time in plant or wooded areas have lower levels of stress hormones, are less likely to be depressed, and have lower blood pressure. Whether your local nature area is in a park or on a mountain, on a boulder, or on the shore, get your bare feet or your seated bottom on the ground for the best meditation ever.

16

THE SEEKER

I have been a seeker and I still am, but I stopped asking the books and the stars. I started listening to the teaching of my Soul.

~Rumi

His Holiness the 14th Dalai Lama wisely said, "Do not go looking for another religion to find enlightenment. The one you were born into, or none at all, will do just fine." Spiritual seekers can be religious, agnostic, or atheist, and there is no need to be another religion to find the answers you seek. Renouncing your religion is not a prerequisite for learning about Spiritual Awakening or Spiritual Enlightenment. Most world religions will lead you to God, and certainly your own relationship to God will lead you there, no matter what name you call him, her, or it.

It is a natural thing to be spiritually curious, and not something we should repress or be ashamed of. Human beings have been seeking connection and unity with their source forever and will continue to do so. Given each human being's unique abilities to sense the physical and spiritual world, each person should be entitled to their curiosity as long as they wish. Our senses are always changing, and we can work to enhance our senses and connections with the physical and spiritual world, so I do not believe that anyone is spiritually disabled; some people are more sensitive to some things than others.

Searching for God and its connection to your spirit is an enduring quest. We are all curious about what we were before we were born, and what really happens after we die, and perhaps most interesting is that not one of us really knows until it happens. It is one of life's great mysteries that I asked as a child and felt religion would answer for me. When I was a baby, my parents had me baptized in a Christian church, but my family had little to offer me on the topic of religion and spirituality. In our living room, however, was a gigantic, large-print, sadistically illustrated, coffee-table sized King James Holy Bible, and this I began to peruse and eventually read by myself, unsupervised, when I was only eight years old. "HOLY BIBLE" was written large in capitals across the cover with a portrait of white Jesus in a long flowing white robe with long flowing dark hair. The full color illustrations depicting many of the famous scenes from the Bible piqued my interest, as would a history book of one's family tree, drawing me more into the story with holy promises that my personal life, death, and redemption would be revealed unto me in full glorious color. (Why a child would ever need redemption perplexed me!) While I was enthralled every evening to open this book and read more clues to link me to a personal Lord and Savior, one picture in particular terrified me and gave me recurring nightmares I dealt with into adulthood. It was a painting of God throwing the Archangel Lucifer into hell, which I interpreted as a kind of eternal prison if one disobeyed God. And since I was a strong-willed child, my "disobedience" was frequent, and I feared that God would be the one to put an end to me, sooner rather than later.

Where I lived in north Orange County, California, in the 1980s there were no other religious options for me of which I was aware other than Christianity. I only knew two kids in my whole school who were Jewish, and I was disappointed to find out that I had to be born into a Jewish family to be Jewish. I already had the Torah at the front of my Bible, but I was never invited to a synagogue, so I was out of luck. With no internet or social media, the Christian bible was my only available research book for spirituality, and I treated it as such. I took notes as I had learned to do in school when searching for an answer in a textbook. Over the months and years, I moved through the table of contents and appendices in my free time searching feverishly for the answer to, "What happens to us when we die?", "Where did I come from?", and "What is my purpose here?"

My confusion about who or what God is stemmed from my feeling at the time that I lacked intellect or study skills, because I was told by so many people that all the answers were in that Holy Book, and faith would help me understand it. I had faith that I would find my answer, but it wasn't faith in the tenets of religion: it was faith that I knew The Way. I knew The Way, because it was already shown to me when I was six, but I had grown to doubt myself as we often do when society makes it clear that children don't know much. Although I already knew a great deal about God through intuition, the existence of established religion made me feel that someone else had a better club I should belong to. Since every person I met said that Christians know God, it seemed to me that belonging to this religion would give me a better education about God. So, I joined the club.

It really was the age-old teenage problem of being afraid of not fitting in that kept me hooked, because all of my friends, all of my community, and for all I knew most of the world belonged to this Christian club. I memorized scripture, sang the hymns, and could tell you all the Bible stories, but none of it made me feel closer to the answer of my three primal questions. I didn't tell anyone until I was in college, at the age of 32, at my final presentation in my final religion class that I had finally decided with all due respect to renounce my Christian faith.

My biggest reason for losing my religion was that it just didn't satisfy my heart's desire for inclusivity. It also relieved me of personal responsibility for my actions with the promise of heaven for just believing in a savior. I personally had so much work to do on myself, I felt I would be setting myself back lifetimes of incarnations if I put my karma on the shoulders of someone or something else. I needed accountability, and I felt it was my personal job to create healing, harmony, and restitution with the Earth and my fellow humans. I figured that if I didn't work out my issues myself, I would never learn what was necessary to earn my healing and achieve my higher purpose.

I feel that God is much greater than any one religion can hold. I feel free to enjoy the process of spiritually evolving and connecting with God and people without the pressure of religious debate. Upon further reflection, I was able to understand the Bible as a story about a beneficent man called Jesus, who took The Hero's Journey and guided my heart, but his connection with the Old Testament God who wiped out the world with a huge flood when he was displeased at humanity would forever mystify me.

When I opened up to a broader view of God and understood the function of religion, I was free to not judge myself or anyone for their choice and practice of religion, and started loving myself without the need for approval or belonging to a religion. When I stepped onto a borderless path of truth unbound by one religion, I found that a great many people were on a similar path and I found my tribe. I read and listened and inquired and learned about some interesting new words and concepts like nirvana, enlightenment, yoga, meditation, chakras, and a funny foreign symbol called OM. I read everything I could get my hands on to learn other accounts of spiritual journeys by counselors, guides, monks, and meditation masters. I realized my gift and learned why I am here. I undoubtedly needed to take the long road to validate my own unique experience, discover my higher purpose on my own, and earn the very peace in my heart. Inner peace is a gift you cannot buy peace or persuade people to give to you; it has to be earned. The work that you do to get that inner peace is the way toward your higher purpose.

17

BRAVELY INTO THE WORLD

Countless people have had spiritual awakenings and were completely overwhelmed by what they saw. They could not bear to see what the world is really like and their participation in the whole horrid dance of humanity. They sometimes turn to drugs, alcohol, or food to numb the pain of having to see their nearest and dearest rejecting their values of peace and love, not to mention the isolation and rejection from others. Being mindful *and* highly sensitive can feel overwhelming. It can be tempting to want to stay in a safety bubble, hide in our bed, attack it with elaborate rituals, or put your head in the clouds and ignore it. While some quiet time will provide you with essential self-care, isolation will not benefit you or anyone else in the long run. Isolating yourself will not make you feel better, and does nothing to increase compassion or harmony in the world. For compassion to blossom, we must acknowledge our ignorance which precedes the wisdom.

If the people surrounding you are not nourishing your need for support, you will naturally feel like an outsider. People don't feel healthy and connected when they feel like an outsider all the time, so the next step is to seek support. Everyone needs and wants support. What you are a part of is a collective of awakened people who are organizing and gaining acceptance like never before in history.

Despite how hideous humanity looks from your mainstream local news channel, enlightening people are nearing a critical mass to bring healing to themselves and the planet. There is no better time to be alive as more people are awakening to raise the collective consciousness!

Your task is to remain calm and create harmony where you can. Keep calm, do your inner work, and carry on. You're going to have to get over the fact that most people do not yet see things as you do, and I encourage you to view this as a benefit, a blessing, a gift. Having been through the fire, you now have two perspectives where most people only have one. You know first-hand what it feels like to be disconnected, distracted, and ignorant. You also know what it feels like to pass through the Gate of Suffering toward greater connection, compassion, and wisdom. Although there may be many days you wish you could go back to living in blissful ignorance, it's better to face the fact that you have been changed for the better. You are a part of a spiritual tribe now—a soul tribe—and I ask you to have faith that you will be, sooner or later, a beacon of light for others to receive connection and healing.

Thankfully, not every person's awakening is accompanied by crisis. Awakening can be a sweet blessing that comes graciously and gradually, waking you up each and every morning with a renewed sense of energy and purpose. I couldn't wish you a sweeter enlightenment than one that occurs over the course of seasons and years with an abundance of support and quiet healing time. I would also wish that your new realizations are validated and accepted by someone you trust, or a supportive group of people who love and accept you for who you are. This is your soul tribe.

A soul tribe is a group of people who share similar beliefs and experiences that further a greater cause. These are people you meet where you just feel a connection, and sense that something bigger is conspiring between you for a greater purpose. "Practice any art . . . no matter how well or badly, not to get money and fame, but to experience becoming, to find out what's inside you, to make your soul grow," wrote the great author Kurt Vonnegut about finding a soul tribe in his book, "Cat's Cradle." A soul tribe can inspire and encourage you while you are becoming, feeding your spiritual energy with nourishing relationships, and make transformational changes with the support of people who are on this journey with you.

In addition to a soul tribe, positive outcomes significantly improve for physical and emotional healing when one is receiving support at home. We are most in need of support by our loved ones, but it you are unlikely to receive it there, therapists, spiritual midwives, energy workers, and other professional healing relationships are essential. Support for your journey can be found in your tribe as well as your family, but family—especially the one you live with—rely on you being a certain way in order to know what to expect from you. As you are healing and changing, they also will need to change how they relate to you.

We all have a face that we hide away forever, and we take it out and show ourselves when everyone has gone.

~Billy Joel

Most people operate mainly from an unconscious mind. Most people are on auto-pilot and the choices about what to have for breakfast and how to get through the day are generally a routine or habit that doesn't take much thought. Spending more time in mindfulness and yoga starts to change your mind, opening energy pathways, and this can change your views and your habits, which sooner or later changes relationships. Because *you* are changing. A seeker wants to be aware, and wants transformation in their lives. But not everyone you know will understand why you are changing or seeking transformation.

The unconscious or un-awakened mind is like a house with many individual sealed rooms within it. These rooms are like having multiple television sets in your house going on in different rooms in your mind. Sometimes the rooms are dark, or the t.v. sets aren't on, or there's just white-noise, but each of these compartments contain all the programming that are the sum total of your experiences and learned behavior here on Earth. In some cases, stored information from past lives is also contained in the mind—some people keep their memories in the living room, some deep down in the basement. These mental compartments contain all the humor of a television sitcom, tragedy of a horror movie, and delusion and embarrassment of an afternoon talk-show, complete with scripts and blocking and a diverse cast of characters of which you play every single role. These compartments contain the rehearsed reactions for a variety of life situations, from which you can unconsciously operate and go about your day to day life. The more time you spend in mindfulness, the doors to these rooms start to open into each other. Some people claim to not even know their house *has* an attic or basement because they are only live in the dining room! Your "house" may end up with a completely open floorplan, while your neighbor has a television screen playing a different show in every room. It's no wonder that these neighbors may have troubles getting comfortable in each other's houses!

It's time to take the mask off and show the people closest to you who you really are. We still need connection and to live in the world with other people. If everyone is wearing a mask, how can we be authentic with each other? How can we be authentic with ourselves? Of what use is meditation if you can't relate to other people? How fun is it at dinner parties to constantly judge others inwardly for their old-fashioned, unenlightened beliefs? You might feel downright sick at how irresponsible people can be toward their health, the products they buy, and the silly commercial customs in which they oblige themselves to participate, but they have their own path to walk. You can pretend that you don't know what being on that side of the fence is like now that you're working on having an open floor plan, but the reality is that you were in the dark once. A selective memory of the past is one way we try to exempt ourselves from the fault of ignorance just because we now have more knowledge and experience about something than others.

One distinctly unconscious activity that is going on all the time in the compartments of our mind is that none of the characters talk to each other. When the mind is not consciously aware, and silent (or not-so-silent) criticisms arise, they sit in these compartments waiting for their air-time, saying their lines according to the way the character was designed by the powerful influences of family up-bringing, trauma, tragedy, society. What a shock it is to hear your own parent's voice coming out of you to criticize someone else! Yes, their opinions are in those compartments, too, because you learned them while you were growing up.

Each of these characters is a part of ourselves, but we should be open to hearing what they have to say about our beliefs and be-havior, pointing to how we acquired those beliefs. Key in shifting your thoughts toward compassion is becoming aware that you like-ly have these compartmental sitcoms going on inside your mind. Raising individual awareness is one responsibility we all have as members of the Human Race. We are all emerging into Lightness of Being.

Although going through a natural transition while you create new boundaries and paradigms for your life, the people closest to you now may not accept this change very easily. New paradigms and boundaries establish personal power and freedom for your life and changes interpersonal dynamics. Some examples of behav-iors and attitudes going through dramatic changes are daily habits or outward appearance, adopting strict meditation practice and prayer, becoming verbally expressive of inner thoughts and feel-ings, or compassionate awareness of ecological preservation. People who have great awareness of the interconnectedness of human and animal life may stop using disposable plastic in favor of reusable bottles; an avid carnivore may stop eating animals and become a vegan, wearing no leather or feathers, may try to impose their new behaviors onto others. An extrovert may behave more introverted or an emotionally steady person may become moody. Maybe you were a permissive person before, and now you want to hold clearer boundaries with people which will bring a notable change to your relationships. A supportive and accepting family is a huge benefit to everyone as they learn and grow, and there is no guarantee they will adapt at the same pace, but sometimes they do. In fact, sometimes one family member's awakening can inspire and instigate changes in many areas of the family's functioning including improved communication, improved health, and even positively influencing purchasing choices that support the environment.

I was quite fortunate to have a few family members who were patient and kind with me as I grew into my new awareness. They called me regularly to see if I was okay, and suggested different kinds of help when I was in crisis. Their love carried me through the hard times. There were others who asked a lot of questions in order to better understand me. And there were a few who were overtly critical and labeled me in a box called "weird hippie." I included them all in my lovingkindness meditations as I recalled the truth of my own ignorance to awaken my compassion for them which assisted me on my healing journey.

There are many good feelings that can come from having a spiritual awakening, and most people would agree that these sound like amazing, joyful experiences! Who *wouldn't* want to feel the internal peace that comes from feeling oneness with all things? Or feel the cosmic support that comes from pure union and connection to the universe? If you think a hug from a loved one feels good, a hug from every atom in the universe feels stellar! A smooth awakening can take place over the course of many years, even decades, and never cause a serious dysfunction in a person's life. I was very fortunate to have a relatively long awakening that occurred in stages and plateaus, and is still evolving to this day.

There are many, less positive feelings that come from having an abrupt spiritual crisis. Perhaps you are disillusioned and feel out of place in this superficial world that doesn't reward you for being in touch with your True Self. Your emotions are constantly on high, feeling too much of everything from everyone, and empathy is slowly killing you. You're tired of hearing people's complaints and feeling that everyone must be stupid because everyone points fingers and no one fixes their problems. You feel fortunate (perhaps even privileged) to live in America, but you're not feeling the love, justice, or equality. You're sick to death that large corporations, political parties, and mega-churches are stacking the deck in their favor, often neglecting the people they claim to serve and employ.

Many people will jump up and enthusiastically take sides with complaint about our modern society. Agreeing with any of these points does not make anyone better than anyone else, but wanting to change your participation in them does make a huge difference. If you recognize feelings of grief and sadness at the magnitude of suffering the world, resist the urge to empathically absorb it or conquer it single-handedly. Don't try to do it all at once. Spiritual awakening and growth is a life-time endeavor, and I don't recommend jumping to action at first impulse, or lying down to give up on everything. There is a middle way.

Recognize your participation in the world without blame or judgment to see specifically the views you hold, or held in the past, and your actions that may have contributed to some conflict. Call this the "taking responsibility" phase of your transformation. Omitting this step will cause a sense of hubris and inflated ego, because it is too easy to make a quick jump to the winning side and cut ties entirely with who you once were. It's convenient to avoid the deep personal work in between stages of awareness, but it is crucial to understand the ignorance that preceded the wisdom.

When you realize how much you've changed during your transformation you might feel guilt, shame, judgmental, in denial, confused, helpless, or threatened. As you recognize your past or present participation in an ethical dilemma, the next step is forgiving your past ignorance and then taking steps to improve future actions and do the same for others. This is not a time to judge others for their unenlightened views; you may recall that it was not too long ago that you did things you are not proud of. Teach without criticizing. This is the time to compassionately bridge the gap between who you were and who you are.

This early in the journey, don't spend your time preaching to others about how to change. Make peace with yourself, because you will indeed discover just how ignorant you were at one time about a lot of things. This is normal. It will take time, but as you recognize the patterns of change, forgive yourself for what came before so that you can heal and move forward. In your meditations, spend some time forgiving and releasing what has come before, and open to compassion for yourself and others to turn a new leaf.

There are many examples of cultural and environmental issues that affect all humanity that we can influence through individual awakening. One universal example that is affecting all of us is human influence on climate change. Perhaps you drive a car that is powered by gasoline, a fossil fuel that when burned emits carbon monoxide and other toxic gases into the atmosphere. Research points to the over usage of fossil fuels and their toxic by-products emitted by cars which are a major influence on weather patterns, also known as climate change. Climate change is a complex issue, but if you believe that human activity makes a difference, such as driving gasoline-powered automobiles, is a part of the problem, we can make a choice that will either contribute to the problem, or contribute to a solution. Because we have freedom of choice in transportation, there are several ways to view our participation in this issue. We could deny that a problem exists. We can deflect the problem by making it someone else's responsibility such as blaming others with even larger waste emissions such as large corporations or even other countries. Or you can try to be a part of the solution. When it comes time to buy a different car, make a different choice such as buying an electric or hybrid, public transportation, or any other number of non-toxic alternatives up to and including not owning a car. Each of these options can be done with or without blaming others, but only personal responsibility and individual action contribute to a solution.

Another example of a social and environmental problem is how people view the use of animals for food or entertainment. Some people consider eating animals their God-given right, and others consider it unnecessary, undesirable, or cruel. What a person eats and how they prepare it is influenced mainly by culture and upbringing, not through conscious decision making, but our views can change through awareness of what animals think and feel that may be contrary to our traditions, habits, and culture. Being more aware of how others think and feel is a strong catalyst to many changes in our families and in our lifestyles. When awareness comes that an animal is a sentient being that has feelings, relationships, and is not a nutritious choice for human health in most cases, there is an opportunity to make a different choice. Depending on the availability of food options in your area and your knowledge of human nutrition, you more than likely have a say in the matter up to and including growing some of your own food, supporting health food restaurants, encouraging business owners to provide healthy options, and shopping at stores that sell sustainable and cruelty-free products.

It does no good to be paralyzed, in denial, or punishing yourself or others about choices made in the past. The choices you make are based on how you think and feel now. What's in the past is past and there's no need to insult anyone who does not feel the way you do. Provide an example for transformation. An enlightened response is remembering that you were once a part of the group that perpetuated suffering, and resolve to make new choices based on what you believe to be the right thing. Then maybe invite your neighbors and family to enJOY a tasty, nutritious, meal made with love, seasoned with real human connection.

18

I WANT TO BE HAPPY: NETTA'S STORY

I was diagnosed with a rare, stage-four cancer under my tongue. I didn't know it was there until I was hospitalized for nine days with pneumonia, and tests came back with this devastating news. My body was so weak I could not walk unassisted around the hospital ward or shower by myself. I was sick for almost 15 years before that hospitalization but I faltered on making any significant changes to improve it. If I hadn't started to change my eating three months before the diagnosis, I might not have even survived the pneumonia.

After the long bout of pneumonia, I got some additional tests which revealed that the cancer had already metastasized. I was told by the doctors to go home and make arrangements to see people before I got too sick to travel. I went to five different oncology hospitals and it boiled down to, at best, just a few years to live. Their treatment suggestions were to remove my tongue and put in a feeding tube and a breathing tube, and I would never be able to speak or eat on my own again. Another doctor said there were no treatment options, that it wouldn't matter what they did. Each appointment was more horrendous than the last.

When I got diagnosed, there are all these crazy things that go through your head like, "I never need to buy shoes again!" and "I never need to go to the dentist again!" One day as we're driving, my husband points out to me, "There's a shoe sale," and I say, "Why would I buy shoes? I'm dying!" It was a 24-hour a day obsession with cancer, researching cancer, treatment options for cancer, and I'm thinking, "God, please give me something else to think about!"

Then I had an epiphany that I didn't want to do any of those medical things. I thought, "I can fix this myself!" Then I thought that I must be so arrogant to think I can fix this myself, but I wanted to beat this. I want to beat this with food, yoga, meditation, and love in my life. I had just started eating for my health, but actually feeling better made me think that I can actually do this. The doctors were suggesting what I felt was an early death that would precede my physical death, and that wasn't okay with me. I had already witnessed first-hand what cancer treatments can do to a person. I know what it's like to be left behind; I know what it's like to want to die when a loved one dies, and I don't want my family to feel like that. I wanted us to be happy as long as possible.

Almost two weeks after I got the diagnosis, I went on a three-week Bucket List Tour around the country visiting family and friends. It was long carefree days with blue sky and wind in my hair, stopping to spend a day or two in each person's home. One day we're driving all over southern Missouri in the back of our friend's van they called "The Shaggin' Wagon." We're out having a great time antique shopping and listening to Wham! and I'm thinking, "I want to live again! The things that used to bug me—why do I hold onto them? I have to be here and be happy!" And that's when I knew that things would be different when I got home. I knew in my heart that I was free of whatever labels the doctors put on this illness, and that I was going to do whatever I could to enjoy whatever time I have left.

Before we left on The Bucket List Tour, I had called a lot of friends and family, one of which was my brother whom I hadn't seen in a very long time. We had let a lot of time elapse since we connected, and he'd never shared much about his personal life nor his career in the U.S. military. Following a series of unfortunate life events, he confessed that he was losing his house. He had served since he was 17 years old, was a Green Beret and a highly decorated veteran, and was so shocked and helpless that the government wouldn't help him to save his home. My brother started opening up to me to share his suffering as a veteran, his injuries and broken life, and not getting help from the government to save his house.

At this point I was still feeling weak, sick, and pretty scared, but I made a video to share what I'm facing and explain my dying wish, and shared it on social media with links to donate. This inspired my brother to make a video, too, which took him six weeks to finish, line by line of what they did to him. The best part is that people really care and are giving money to this man they've never met before. People are going through their own crises, and now they have hope. They are thanking me for sharing and giving and loving, simply because it's my dying wish. My brother has hope now, too, and says to me, "I think you may have saved my life!"

I feel like I'm living my own funeral and hearing my own eulogy. All these wonderful connections have come from this. People are coming out of the woodwork—classmates, siblings, cousins who haven't spoken to me in 20 or 30 years are talking again—not only because I have cancer, but because I decided I want to do something big and important while I'm alive. There is some urgency in knowing that you might die soon, and I think they are feeling it from me, wanting to do something good and memorable too.

But I couldn't have started any of this if I didn't feel so much better because I was eating better, and I certainly couldn't have continued this journey. I started changing my eating habits about three months before the diagnosis, but every meal nowadays I just feel better and better—with yoga and my smoothies, and the love and support I'm getting every day—I feel I can keep this going. I see how other people react to being sick, or getting a dreaded diagnosis. They give up or beat themselves up over it, but most people's biggest fear is having regret that you didn't help the people you wanted to help, or spend more time doing the things that matter most to you. Taking care of your health is one of the biggest things you can do to ensure you can give, serve, and love. I had to decide that I *wanted* to feel better.

Then when I realized I had enough energy to mobilize people to connect and help each other, it took on a life of its own. I started concentrating on this project, and realized just how lucky I am to have a great support system. I love this feeling of being a part of something bigger than myself, but I don't want to get attached. I have to remember that I may have bad times again. My husband and I have been through some hard, hard times this year, yet I am the happiest I have ever been.

Perhaps I could have saved myself a lot of headaches by making changes earlier, but we can't go back in time to change anything. I could not see what I could not see. It took getting cancer to make me see what I could not see before, so that is all a process of awakening. It happened in the way it needed to happen to get my attention, to change my diet, to travel to hospitals and hear the awful things they were planning for my treatment. I was not satisfied at all with the dim and painful quality of life that was my brief future if I accepted all of their invasive solutions. At almost the same point that I accepted what had become of my health, I knew at that moment that I was going to change it. I accepted it and released attachment to it right away so I could do as much as I could with the time I have left. I made rapid and essential dietary changes which led me to feeling better and better, and I'm still feeling the improvement daily! I didn't know way back when that my health had declined so much over the years, but feeling better every day still helps me see how much more I can do no matter what happens. I have made more of a dramatic shift in my health in such a short time than I ever thought possible.

Improved relationships and the diet have changed how I feel about everything. I didn't realize how much pain I was in until the pain was gone, and I don't want the pain to come back. I have mobilized people into doing something greater than them, and they are calling me to thank me for giving them a purpose. If it wasn't for cancer, I wouldn't have raised money for my brother. If it wasn't for cancer, my husband may not have changed his diet also. If it wasn't for cancer, I might not have gone on a Bucket List Tour and realized I wanted to have a happy life, not merely a longer life, so this was all quite a blessing.

19

THE GIFT

I slept and dreamt that my life was joy.
I awoke and saw that life was service.
I acted and behold, service was joy.

~Rabindranath Tagore

At the end of a hatha yoga practice, we lay down in savasana, known as corpse pose, to abide in the inner peacefulness that is the culmination of yoga. Many people eagerly anticipate this respite at the end of a physical practice because they take rest. At its deepest level, savasana is much more than rest. It the practice of a once-in-a-lifetime experience: a sort of mimicked death. We lay down on the floor for 5 to fifteen minutes to rest from the physical practice, but the real reason behind it is to help us prepare for the inevitable ending of our life with our last breath. When we lay down with mindfulness, it is as if the ground itself has come up to support us. We cease to control our movements, our breath, our thoughts, and our emotions, the things that cause us to live purposefully, and allow the involuntary processes of the body take over. In our practice, we know consciously that we are able to get back up from the ground and continue our day, but in the last day, our last breath, we will not. There will be no more struggles. We abide in stillness to free the mind and body from the attachment and expectation that life is eternal, and we find bliss. There is no more work to be done at that moment. There is nothing we need to do or plan. In this sacred practice we let go of everything in preparation for the final moment when the breath does not come into our body again, and we can be at peace with nothing unsettled, no longing, and no regret. The gift of the practice of savasana and of yoga itself is an open-hearted gratitude for our precious time here, and a blissful feeling that all is well in this moment. We accept with reverence and gratitude what is here to be experienced in this life and the mystery of what may lie beyond.

When we consider the time we have, no matter whether for a day, a minute, or a century, we must make time for compassion, gratitude, acceptance, and fun. Learn from your suffering and ignorance how to have great compassion. Be thankful for all the lessons this journey has taught you; hopefully you won't need to endure hard lessons much longer than is necessary for you to learn them. Accept with reverence and gratitude who you are right now and where you are even if you feel a strong calling to change it all immediately. Create pause and rest between the changes. Everything you've experienced has brought you to this moment in the circumstances you find yourself in, for better or worse. And if you keep a wide perspective, you'll notice that on most days there will be a peaceful flow of energy that surrounds you and unrivaled moments of pure bliss. Season your life by enjoying all the seasons of your life. Bear witness to the celestial cycles and earthly seasons. The daily appearance of the sunrise and sunset seem unchangeable, but you will change each day. Get silly sometimes and enjoy a good laugh regularly. Spiritual growth shouldn't be all serious; in fact, some realizations are downright hilarious! Find beauty in the shifting, the transitions, everything, especially yourself. These are the moments that you can string together, breath by breath, minute by minute, in ritual sacred experience that makes a regular life feel simply extraordinary

Pursue your dreams as they are revealed to you one small step at a time, but find time daily to be in the moment. When you have time and energy to do more, do just one thing, and be present as you do that one thing. When you open to using your gifts to do even more, be in that moment, too. Every moment will unfold into the next as you integrate your awakening in to a more purposeful, enjoyable life. Start planting the seeds of your future in the moment you are in now.

As your strength and patience increases, help someone. Life is most fulfilling when we have used our time and resources to help someone do something that they could not have done themselves. This could be providing the raw materials to create or grow something, or it could be using someone else's resources to create something that helps people. On the most basic level, helping someone else achieve or experience something they could not have done for themselves is why we are all here. We all have knowledge to share, skills to teach, and comfort to give, and in time you will also be the recipient of such. This, too, is a gift. And when you accept what others have to offer, in the end, you will provide a precious opportunity for someone else to share, teach, and comfort you. When you have a little extra energy and faith that it will carry on for some time, consider what is possible to do with this one precious life. After the raging fire of awakening and healing, what seeds will bloom in your next season? Each individual must decide for themselves whether they're going to just be happy in the moment, ride on the coat-tails of fate, or get inspired do something they previously thought was impossible.

Take great interest in your health and level of contentment. Make your happiness a priority (not the only priority, of course), and this will bring happiness to yourself and those who truly love you. Take interest in your own health and wellbeing; this will inspire others who are ready to do the same. Compassionate actions will become a natural extension of you and a big part of your daily routine so that filling your own cup first and enjoying whatever is in it will never detract from the cups of your friends, family, and community. When you are refreshed, your wellbeing and happiness will increase.

There are no wrong choices, just the choice that is right for you. Aside from helping yourself feel better, there are 7 billion people on this planet to provide help, guidance, and comfort. We can be inspired by the stories shared here to find meaning and greater purpose in the caretaking of deep connections that we already share. We are all sparks of God, and each effort we make to be in connection with our Source helps the universe expand with harmony. Every action makes a ripple in the big pond of humanity, extending farther and wider than we can ever imagine, but we don't really need to look further than our own backyard for a place to throw some pebbles. It is my hope that you will feel supported and encouraged in pursuit of whatever dreams may come to you.

Your healing journey is to realize your connection to God, and to give a sparkle of Light from God to humanity however you can. Your gifts and special senses are a part of you and should be enjoyed like the rest of your senses, utilized in your work and leisure. Your gifts can be carried on to help, to educate, to share, or to serve in a special way, *your* way. The more you practice self-care and self-study, you will discover more about your natural gifts and ways to use them. I've always felt there's some reason for the fashion in which my healing journey has evolved. Something inside of me said that I was to go in this direction or that direction, and when I listened to that guidance, things went a lot better for me. My suffering was a great teacher of love and compassion for myself and others, and learning to listen to Spiritual guidance was another important lesson. My task is to embrace my gifts, strengthen them, and enJOY them so that my work and leisure are both gratifying.

It is my wish that every human being is able to gently awaken to their Divine connection and learns to accept their highly sensitive nature as an extension of the Divine. I hope that you will embrace your role as a communicator and connector of the Divine with all life, seen and unseen, known and unknown. Our journey of suffering, healing, and integration is not merely a singular experience by one sentient individual, but a collective experience of an entire sentient universe. The suffering of one part is a suffering of the whole, yet the healing of one person can lead to the healing of many others. Our tribe is growing, and you are a part of it. Do not squander this life. There is no more time for self-pity, guilt, or shame. Complete your healing journey and shine on!

The gift of awakening is finding your way back to the whole through the healing journey and connecting to God through compassion of all sentient beings. Another gift is learning to love and accept yourself wholly as a spark of the Divine with all of your special senses and quirky oddities. The compassion and forgiveness we extend in the face of ignorance, anger, and greed will encourage many and more to do the same, uniting us in harmony despite our differences. We are all connected as One. We are a gift to each other.

Made in the USA
Columbia, SC
05 May 2018